DON'T WORRY ABOUT THE MULE GOING BLIND

Don't Worry About The Mule Going Blind

Jean
Wishing you
success on your
creative
Journey

An American Story

Betty Tucker

Betty Tucker

4/4/2024

510 260 4618

To my twins, Sonia Denise Jones and Tonya Denise Jones

CONTENTS

PREFACE

I wrote this book to share with readers a few things I hold true: Whatever you believe, you can achieve. No matter how difficult, your circumstances do not define who you are. Resilience, hard work, and openness to change will carry the day. When you know better, you do better. You always have options. Regardless of what you're going through, your situation is not permanent. Whatever is going on, it is there to teach you how to acquire the skills you need to grow.

This book is, in part, about the circumstances of my childhood. I grew up in debilitating poverty, borne of racism: exploitive migrant labor, multiple rapes and other abuse, chronic illness among my family and acquaintances ... the list is long and bitter. And yet I have found that these circumstances do not define who I am. I have gone beyond them.

I want to show teens and women in particular that with a heartfelt, sincere, and honest approach they can create a life beyond their wildest dreams. The purpose of this book is to demonstrate, using the example of my life, that you should never give up your dream of a better life, that you can make what you believe into your reality. I believed that I deserved better, I relentlessly pursued it with all my heart, and it became real. My hope is that through this book, I can share the tools that keep me motivated and steadfast in my determination for a better life.

My hope for you is that you are, even now, developing the tools you need to conquer the demons, in yourself and in those around you, that hinder your right to live a life of your choosing. I want to provide you with an empowering challenge to live a better life.

You—yes, you—are engineered for greatness. You're programmed to succeed. You don't have to have a GPS, MapQuest, or OnStar. All you need is faith, action, and a belief in your self-worth, and you're already half-way to your destination.

I want to thank my developmental editor, Patricia Heinicke Jr., who encouraged, inspired, and motivated me to share my journey. This book would have never been possible without her help. I want to thank my five children who stood by me while I struggled as a parent and a mother, who never gave up the belief that their mother is special and deserves to fulfill her destiny. I will forever be grateful to the Warrens, who believed in me when I doubted my own uniqueness. And I thank you, dear reader, for picking up this book.

INTRODUCTION

In the next few chapters, you will read about my experience as a child migrant worker in New York and Florida. Now when most Americans hear "migrant worker," they imagine people of Mexican descent picking tomatoes in California, not African Americans picking beans and cutting sod in Florida. So I'm going to lay out a few facts to help get you oriented.

I did much of my growing up in Belle Glade, Florida, a place that came into public view back in 1960, with Edward R. Murrow's documentary on migrant workers called Harvest of Shame. The film shows what life was like in Belle Glade when I lived there.

But the history of this region as an agricultural center goes back to before the 1940s, when African Americans were heavily recruited to come to Florida to cut sugar cane. Advertisements targeted to black Americans offered good work on the plantations of the United States Sugar Corporation, with free transportation to Florida, good wages, good living conditions, and free housing and medical care.

But it was a bait and switch. Workers were trapped on the plantations for the duration of their contract, forced to pay back the cost of their "free" transportation, or charged high prices for their "free" rent and for food and drink available to them only at a company store. Many soon became indebted to the company because their store charges were more than their pay. The U.S. Sugar Corporation essentially coerced the farmworkers to remain on site, some against their will, and eventually the company was brought to task. In 1942, U.S. Sugar was indicted for conspiracy to hold black sugar cane workers in peonage (essentially involuntary servitude, a.k.a. slavery). The company responded by no longer hiring African Americans, giving the excuse that the locals "didn't want" the sugar cutting jobs. To get around the new labor requirements, in 1943 they started importing people from Jamaica.

Meanwhile, Belle Glade became known as the "Winter Vegetable Capital of the World," and black workers who no longer found work in the sugar fields found it on the Florida truck farms, picking and processing crops. This is the type of work my family did, both in New York and in Florida. As you will see, our experiences as migrant workers had an incalculable impact on the rest of our lives.

Unfortunately, many things are still unchanged in Belle Glade. In 1985, almost twenty years after I left there, the town was still notorious for its poverty. According to a New York Times report in April of that year, Belle Glade had the highest rate of HIV infections per capita in the nation. Although over 50 percent of the housing in Belle Glade at that time was substandard and 20 percent of the buildings were classed "uninhabitable," residents used all of it because little new housing was being built. In 1990, Stephanie Black's documentary H-2 Worker revisited Belle Glade (the film went on to win the Grand Jury Prize at the 1990 Sundance Film Festival). This film surveyed the history of the region and investigated the current labor practices, which continued to be exploitive. The U.S. Congress was hearing testimony on conditions in Belle Glade as recently as 2008. In 2009 over 60 percent of the population lived beneath the poverty level, and nearly 20 percent lived at or below 50 percent of the poverty level (See "Belle Glade, Florida: Poverty Rate Data," at www.city-data.com/poverty/poverty-Belle-Glade-Florida.html). Many people still live without electricity or indoor plumbing.

Clearly the legacy of slave and migrant labor is long-lived here, and I hope that my story will bring some of this legacy to light. But more importantly, I hope it will inspire you to see beyond your circumstances, no matter how desperate, and to pay attention to what is truly powering your decisions. Perseverance and faith are important, but they are not enough; you also need a continual openness to self-knowledge. "When you know better, you do better," and there's no time like the present to start.

Life is always about choices. Even as a baby, you've got choices to make about how to get what you want. Of course, at that stage it's pretty simple: if you want to be held, fed, changed, or just have your position altered, you yell and hope that someone can understand you. But as you grow older you negotiate with yourself about the choices you're going to make to get what you want. And a lot more goes into what approach you're going to use to obtain your objective. Most of the time you are aware only of the objective; it takes a certain maturity to have a plan.

The one thing that doesn't always involve choice is the people you allow to enter your heart.

One of my current heart-throbs is my grandson, Javian. When his father, my son George, accepted a job out of the area and came home only occasionally, I began to keep Javian, who at the time was a headstrong two-year-old, for two or three days a week. At first, the boy would have nothing to do with me. The only people he allowed near him were his parents and his maternal grandmother. The first time his mother dropped him off at my place, he stood at the door for hours, pulling on the door knob and crying endlessly. He did not want me to be near him or even to touch him.

It went on from there. The more fun activities I planned for him, the more he seemed to resent me. And the more time I spent with him, the more I loved him! He reminded me of George at that age—headstrong and independent. For example, when George was two years old, he potty trained himself by going to the bathroom with the rest of us at every opportunity to see what we were doing. And when George was in kindergarten, he wanted to walk to school by himself, and he insisted that he could take care of himself and did not need a babysitter.

As we became better acquainted, I began to see that Javian, like his father, wanted to do everything for himself. During our daily walk, he wanted to push the stroller down the steps. He wanted to select what clothing to put on; he wanted to decide what he wanted for breakfast; he wanted to plug in the vacuum when I vacuumed. In fact, throughout the day he would say, "I want to help you! Let me help you!" Whenever I took the garbage out he would demand a garbage bag to take out himself. When we went to bed, he would demand to turn the lights and TV off himself. Gradually, we began to get along.

Every night we would read two or three bedtime stories and I would lay with him until he fell asleep. Then, over time, some nights he would say, "I want to sleep on the pillow with you." Other times, he would ask me to hold his hand as he fell asleep. Those requests just melted my heart because they showed pure love: something that you feel inside that you have no control off. I was in love, through no decision of my own.

But love brings choices with it. Some are easy, and some are hard.

Another person in my heart is Ms. Johnnie Mae, who at this writing is ninety-three and in the last stages of Alzheimer's. She and Javian couldn't be more different.

I first knew Ms. Johnnie Mae when I was a child in Troy, Alabama, where she was our next-door neighbor. Years later, she would say, "I've known Betty ever since she was a child; she was born on my door step." Back then she worked as a cook for Troy University, and the leftover food she brought home to Ma and Pa helped feed us seven children. After we moved to Florida in 1959, when I was nine years old, it would be a long time before I gave her another thought.

I reconnected with her by accident in 2001. I was visiting my family in Florida, trying to get over a major depression. My sister Catherine invited me to come with them to Troy for the Fourth of July weekend. When we arrived, we stopped at a supermarket, and my cousin Robert pointed to a huge, white, well-groomed home next to the market and said, "Betty, that is Ms. Johnnie Mae's home." And there she was, pruning roses in her yard. At eighty-two, she was just as beautiful and peaceful as the roses she was pruning. I walked up the steep hill and re-introduced myself. At fifty-four years old, I looked like I lived in a second-hand store: wrinkled brown blouse, overworn purple pants, flip-flops that wouldn't stay between my toes, matted black hair with a partial wig covering my sores, very dry burned-black skin, yellow teeth that protruded out of my mouth, with four missing. But I had the poise and speech of a well-educated northern black female.

I stood about two arms' lengths from her and said, "Ms. Johnnie Mae, I'm Hazel and John Owens' daughter, Betty Owens." She drew me closer, gave me a big hug, and said she was sorry to have heard my mother and father had separated. We talked for a bit, and in the middle of our short conversation, she told me that an acquaintance of hers would be staying in her guest house the following month to do research on his family's genealogy. I was immediately intrigued because I was also interested in genealogy and local history; both of my parents were born and raised in Troy. I asked her if she would ask her guest if I could go with him during his research and see how it was done.

It was agreed upon, and the next month I returned to Troy to start my research. I stayed for a week with Ms. Johnnie Mae. I didn't get a lot of research done, but it didn't really matter. The unbelievable hospitality that she showed me as a guest in her home caressed my broken heart.

First, I was in a lot of pain from work-related injuries sustained at the U.S. Postal Service, and tired of having to go the Department of Labor doctors and hear them saying nothing was wrong with me. Second, I was still experiencing grief from losing my sister Johnnie, although I was going to group grief counseling. Third, my Ma had suffered a stroke that had left her completely paralyzed and probably close to brain dead; she could not speak or communicate in any way—all she could do was move her eyes. Fourth, I was feeling the empty nest syndrome; both of my boys had left home: George living in Florida and Greg attending Philander Smith College in Arkansas. And underneath all that was a whole life of struggle and loss.

I realized then how it could be so easy to kill yourself when you're depressed because part of you is whispering in your ear, "Go ahead, drive that car into the brick wall as fast as you can; nothing will happen" or "Jump in front of that BART train; you're not going to get hurt—all the pain will just be over." Whenever you become suicidal, you know you're suffering from severe depression. When I heard that Marie Osmond's son had jumped to his death out of a building, again the voice whispered (that voice that's always there keeping you company), "Go ahead and jump, you'll be all right." It's not a voice you literally hear, not like a psychosis; it's an internal voice that speaks to your mind.

As you will see, my life had basically been like Wipe Out, the reality TV show where contestants compete in a water obstacle course to see who can complete the task in the fastest time. So being around Ms. Johnnie Mae and her son, Eddie B., gave me something I had never experienced. They didn't complain, fuss, or disagree. They enjoyed each day as if it was the first day of their life. They enjoyed each other's company completely, even while doing ordinary things like watching TV or eating dinner. They talked to each other. I felt my life had not been about talking, but about hollering, fussing, cursing, and silence. During my visits with them things were peaceful and serene; I could sit in a recliner and read a book with pleasure and enjoyment. I'd never before experienced that type of peace in my life, and I wanted to be a part of it.

Even in her eighties Ms. Johnnie Mae acted like life couldn't get any better, and here I was thirty years younger and couldn't find beauty in anything. She acted as if she had found the fountain of youth. I wanted to spend as much time as I could around her so I could learn some secret that I thought she knew about life.

Ms. Johnnie Mae had started a Senior Citizens' Travel Club, and that next Christmas she was hosting a Christmas party for the club's members. In return for her hospitality, I told her that I would return and help her with the party.

On the day of the party, I was back in Troy. Ms. Johnnie Mae had cooked a feast fit for a king. The party was scheduled to start at six o'clock in the evening, but some of the guests started showing up before four. By five o'clock, the entire guest list had arrived. We didn't even have time to change into our party attire!

Now I had never entertained a fly. But I somehow took on the persona of a devoted hostess. I treated the guests like they were royalty, assisting them with their every whim. I did not act like that to impress them; I simply wanted to show Ms. Johnnie Mae how much I appreciated her. My goal was to treat the guests like they were important heads of state. I knew it worked because I overheard several of them asking Ms. Johnnie Mae, "Where is that gal from? Who is she?" Then, immediately after the party I began cleaning: washing plates, pots, pans, glasses, spoons, forks, and cups from both of the kitchens and the two dining areas.

When Eddie B. came home late that night, I overheard him tell Ms. Johnnie Mae how spic and span the kitchens and dining areas were. It didn't even look like there had been a regular meal, much less a party! He was impressed.

After that visit, I returned occasionally to Alabama to travel with my new friend on one of her travel club trips, and I stayed with her at least once while Eddie B. was out of state for his yearly two-week military reserve duty. Ms. Johnnie Mae and I began to trust each other and developed a deep love and respect for each other. Eventually I moved in for a longer stay, living with her and her son for two and a half years, from August 2004 through May 2007, and again for several months in 2009. Every time I visited, she welcomed me with open arms.

Over the years, Ms. Johnnie Mae treated me like her daughter, and she was more a mother to me than my own mother had been. She was so loving and joyful, and so gentle and generous with me. At one point Ms. Johnnie Mae said, "Betty, when I get too old to climb the stairs at the big house, we will move to the guest house." The guest house had only one bedroom, plus a kitchen and bath. So I said, "I don't think that will work. How are all three of us going to fit?" So she added another room to the guest house, just so I could have my own bedroom in the future.

I loved our life together. We went out every day except Friday and Saturday, which were our days to rest and kick back. Every Sunday, we went to church. She was a member of several community organizations, and a member of a congressional committee on aging. She participated in fashion shows and was often asked to be a speaker for various community organizations. In other words, we had a busy schedule.

On our daily outings, she was treated as an honorable person, a privilege that she had earned, especially through the civil rights work she had done in the early efforts to register black voters. She have even gone so far as to risk her and her family's lives by allowing northern white college students to live in her home while they recruited black people to register and vote.

Always well groomed, Ms. Johnnie Mae did not leave the house without makeup, and she matched her outfits as if she was competing in a color scheme contest. And her seventeen-room home was always spotless. It fascinated me that anyone at that age could care that much about themselves. I was in awe. I felt the more time I spent around her, witnessing the love she had for herself, the more I would learn how to love myself.

Ms. Johnnie Mae showed me love without wanting anything in return from me except friendship. The love she showed me gave me strength and hope for a better future. I had not felt that type of love since my sister, also named Johnnie Mae, died in 1997.

Upon my return to California in late 2009, I was torn about leaving Ms. Johnnie Mae. But I had my own children and grandchildren, including Javian, to consider. Then in July 2010, she had surgery to repair an aneurism in her stomach.

She was not doing well, and soon thereafter, my inner voice said, "Betty, a promise is a commitment. You had a nonverbal understanding with Ms. Johnnie Mae that you would always be with her, to the end of life, whether you or she goes first. What you will gain by keeping that promise is more than what you will miss. Don't worry about the time you have left on this earth, because you're not the time keeper. God is."

I listened to that voice and moved to Alabama to help with Ms. Johnnie Mae's care. I have never looked back.

So I've made a choice. It feels good. And I think one reason it feels good, much better than other choices I've made, is that I'm stronger and more aware of my options than ever before in my life. One gift Ms. Johnnie Mae has given me is the time and ability to look back at the choices I've made in my life—from those that didn't feel like choices because I didn't know my own freedom to those that were solidly intentional. I've had a chance to look back and think about where I came from and how that has influenced who I've become.

That's what this book is about. I hope you enjoy it.

COUNTRY LIVING

An overbearing oak tree stands in front of our home, standing guard and at attention, holding our lives in its hand. Larger and stronger than our tiny wooden house, it has its own agenda, especially during the winter. Even before the lighting and thundering start in, the tree begins to sway back and forth, warning that it might just fall right on top of us. So it takes only the thought of an approaching storm for Ma to gather all her children and run to a neighbor's more securely built home. Once we arrive at the neighbor's, Ma establishes a mood of sheer terror. As the rain beats on the tin roof, she and the older girls form a circle around the babies in the corner of the main room, praying to survive the unpredictable storm. When Dad arrives home from work on a rainy day, he has to look for his family.

But Johnnie and I are never afraid.

City blacks living in southern Alabama in the 1950s had it worse than the rural blacks, who could at least grow and harvest their own food. In Troy, Alabama, we weren't rural, but it wasn't a steaming metropolis either. We were functional poor—no running water, electricity, or indoor toilet, and we sometimes ran out of food. The only true white person seen in the neighborhood was the insurance man, who showed up once a month.

But my father, John Owens, did support his family, working at a mill from sun up to sun down. Eventually he earned a dollar an hour, which was a good salary, especially for black folks. Every Friday when he got paid, Uncle Pike his sister's husband, took him shopping for groceries at the store owned by the mill owner. Dad gave Ma all the money he had left, and she'd give him fifty cents for a haircut. To supplement his income, Dad dug graves and hunted for possum, squirrels, and other live game.

Dad was born on a farm in Troy, the eldest child of a large family. He grew up to be a very dark, handsome man with eyes that confessed the depth of his soul. When he reached beyond his boundaries and fell unconditionally in love with Ma, his life was no longer his own. His life was Ma.

Hazel, as she was named, had razor-blade blue eyes, with medium-brown olive skin and a stature that could not be reckoned with. Ma was a city girl, the eldest of six children. From what I've been told, Grandpa was paralyzed after falling into a well he was digging. So after Ma graduated from the eleventh grade, she went to work to help support her family instead of pursuing her dream of nursing or teaching school. She worked for a while as a housekeeper for whites, but she couldn't manage being a maid and started eagerly pursuing a mate who would cater to her every whim. She met my dad at a church gathering. They held hands and were soon married.

Then came us kids. Ma always appeared to be satisfied with making babies, which she did like she was making biscuits: whenever they were baked, her job was complete. That is where my sister Sarah's chorus begins: cooking, cleaning, washing, and babysitting.

Sarah was the oldest. There were seven of us: Sarah—who we called Honey Gal—Johnnie, Catherine—nicknamed Bush—Betty, Jab, Sammy, and Ann. And Ma was known to beat Johnnie and me down. I never remember Ma hitting Sarah or Bush or my younger siblings. Sarah was so timid; if Ma said "Come here" to her, she'd immediately start to cry. And Bush was saved from beating by a constant nosebleed from some unknown disease. But if me or Johnnie so much as hesitated when she asked us to do something—sweep the

2

leaves in yard or fetch something—there was a beat down. She'd say, "Come here!" and we'd take off running like we were trying to outrun a bullet. She'd send long-legged Honey Gal to catch us, and she always did; either we got tired and stopped running or she caught us and brought us to Ma. Then Ma would send another child to get a switch off the tree. It didn't matter what we'd done; the whipping was always the same. She'd put our head under an old church chair, with only our naked butt sticking out, and she'd sit on the chair and beat us until she got tired.

Ma worked fast, though. After she got your head and butt properly situated under the chair and got herself sitting in it, the beating lasted for less than two minutes—just like wringing the neck of a chicken you were going to eat for dinner. Chicken or child, you do not tarry. As she beat us, she'd tell us why. Then she would remind us of other things we had done that she did not like. Lying with your head under the chair was like being in a choke hold, and you could have easily passed out. Her licks were hard, with a stick or a broom handle, and after a couple of licks, you couldn't even cry or scream.

Even Dad was cautious of Ma. When he came home after drinking, he'd open the screen door slowly and throw his hat inside onto the floor to determine what type of mood she was in. If Ma didn't say anything, he knew she was in a good mood and felt it was safe to enter. Otherwise, he sat on the porch until he thought she had cooled off. If she started fussing he knew that he was not going to have a good time: Ma would be after him about drinking, talk about how his family was crazy, he was a not good man, he should not be gambling because we needed the money—anything to make him feel less than a man.

So I don't know how Johnnie and I had the nerve to rebel against Ma, but we did. Johnnie always sassed Ma on the run, or under her breath. Like she'd say, "When Dad's get home I'm gonna ask him where I get my color from!" Ma would hear the mumbling, and that was all she'd need for a beat down. But I admired that dare Johnnie had in her, and I was an instigator for her. She was not afraid of anything, not even the dead.

Johnnie's nickname growing up was "Mama." Aunt Juanita gave her this nickname and it stuck because Johnnie was the one who helped Ma talk to white folks whenever she had to go to town to take care of business, and it was Johnnie who helped Auntie with ways to do business in a common-sense way. "Mama, I need you to go with me to the courts to pay a bill," Auntie would say. Then all the details of the transaction had to be discussed, because Johnnie wanted things to go as planned.

She was like a stage actor practicing a scene, even with ordinary things like scheduling the day. Auntie'd say, "Mama, first we're going over my brother Marvin's house to pick up the milk and butter, then we going to pick the berries next." Johnnie would interrupt, "Auntie, why are you going to drive to Uncle Marvin's house first and drive out of your way so we can pick the berries? We should pick berries first, and on our way back, since we got to come that way, we can stop at Uncle Marvin's house to pick up the milk and butter."

"Mama, you have so much sense. You're going to make something of yourself one day."

We were fortunate that our neighbor, Mrs. Johnnie Mae Warren, worked in a school cafeteria and brought the leftover food home for us every day. Her husband, Mr. Ed, had my complexion, and Mrs. Johnnie Mae looked white. Not light-skinned or high yellow, but white. They had a beautiful gated corner home with electric lights, an inside bathroom, and a kitchen with running water. They had a television and a car.

We had two rooms and a kitchen, with a wood stove, a well, and an outhouse out back.

But we had the marbles, and their boy, Eddie B. Warren, was not allowed to crawl on his knees. Still, sometimes when we were in the middle of a game he would come over and demand that we start over so he could play. I never understood how someone could come into your yard and give you orders.

Eddie B.'s baby sister, Elaine, had pink cheeks with dimples and golden Shirley Temple curls. And she was treasured like gold. Elaine used to stand by the fence, calling us names and telling her brother to come home.

Before I was nine years old, I had to have surgery to remove a tissue growing in my eye. I was scared to death. During the surgery, Ma held my hand, telling me that everything was going to be all right and not to cry. She stroked my nappy hair and rubbed my shoulder. My Uncle Marvin drove us home from the hospital, and Ma had him to stop at the store so she could buy me a cookie for being such a good girl. She held my head in her chest and rubbed my arm. It was a comfort.

When I was a small child, mostly my mothering came from Honey Gal, who always treated me as if I was her baby doll. Every morning before school, she heated water on the wooden stove and washed me up and dressed me. Afterwards, she would carry me to the kitchen and force me to eat grits or bread, even though I would raise holy hell and try to keep my mouth shut. When she finished with me, I'm sure she was eager to go to school. Then me and Honey Gal, Ma and Johnnie, Bush, Jab, Sammy and Ann would go to Grandma's house, which was near the school. Walking was something a baby doll did not do, so Honey Gal had to carry me, along with her books. During her walk, I allowed her to put me down only to rest for a few seconds.

When Ma was not with us, we would take a shortcut to Grandma's house—maneuvering through the field and around the stream and the cows. Sometimes the stream overflowed and we'd have to find another place to cross safely. After crossing we entered a thicketed area, draped with long branches and silent leaves.

The quiet lasted only a moment, because the second we lifted our heads out the top of the embankment, the neighbor kids bombarded us with anything they could pick up and throw. Instead of ignoring these children and running, Johnnie would talk back to belittle them for attacking us: "You don't go to school; your clothes is too ragged!" "Your sister is pregnant and not married!" or "You got a big head!" With those kids at least, Johnnie was selling wolf tickets, and I was still afraid to fight. But I didn't have any problem screaming when the going got rough for Johnnie. Usually if we screamed loud enough some adult would come out to see what was going on.

After surviving that encounter, we'd have to pass the witch's house in front of Cousin Fred's. That property looked abandoned; even the house had weeds growing out of it! The witch always wore black, and if she saw any kids walking on the road in front of her house, she ran out her front door with an ax, a hoe, or a butcher knife, yelling obscenities from her porch. So we'd pass her house swiftly and soundlessly, for fear of annoying her.

Finally, we were at Grandma's. Ma felt better over at her ma's house because Auntie Juanita, who lived nearby, took over our care. She'd take all the kids who were not in school, and we'd spend our days with her and her kids—exploring the surroundings, playing house, fighting, searching for gold in a ditch, pretending we were Tarzan, playing marbles. Auntie's house was a child's paradise. She was a hoarder—her house was so full of stuff there was no walking place—and we were allowed to play freely there. Or she would have something planned. She'd pile us all into her old automobile and take us somewhere—like to her brother's farm, where we got milk, cheese, and vegetables. Or we would pick berries or look for chalk on the side of the road, and sometimes we'd go fishing. Auntie was the first entrepreneur I knew; she sold chalk, and she sold bootleg whiskey. She never took her children to church, and she and her husband partied every weekend like a rock stars.

After school, Honey Gal and Johnnie came to Grandmother's house to help Ma carry us home. Once home, Johnnie would fetch wood for the stove; Honey Gal got the kids settled; and Ma started dinner. Bush always sat on the porch with a rag stuffed up her nose to stop the bleeding. I waited for Johnnie to finish her chores so we could play marbles, or when dusk came, play hide-and-seek or look for lightning bugs.

One highlight of our pilgrimages to Grandma's house was going to Cousin Fred's for our weekly ghost story. Cousin Fred was an undertaker, and we believed every word he said.

A lean, muscular man with flawless skin, Cousin Fred brushed a piece of lint from his meticulous black tuxedo as he looked in the mirror. The face in the mirror had the shine of a hand-polished hardwood floor, with not a line visible, just like the palms of his hands. His eyebrows extended across his forehead, with upper and lower lips equally composed. After gently polishing his ears with white powder, he put on long, black gloves with black chicken feathers sticking from the fingers. He bowed as he put on his black

7

wizard's top hat. His boots were hard knobs, with soles so thick they seemed part of the boot.

Charming, kindhearted, and serene, like an unruffled karamu, and the whole formation wrapped with contentment, Cousin Fred opened his door and in walked five children. Honey Gal: chunky, with long, substantial legs and wearing a nurse's hat; Johnnie: daring, bold, unafraid, tomboy of the group, entering with a rush; Bush: alert, frightened, uneasy, dressed in blouse, pants, dress, sweater, coat, scarf with no shoes, looking nervously over her shoulder; Betty: cared-for-younger child, puny as chicken feet; Alto Jr, lanky and awkward, like his dad.

Cousin Fred walked away from the front door, the cape on his shoulder swishing back and forth, to sit, daunting, on the stool before the children, amused by their reaction. Tree branches slammed against the tin roof of the house, and the wind sang a sinister melody. It was spine chilling. The children, petrified, sat in a circle in front of the fireplace. Cousin Fred gave each of them one of his famous homemade chocolate chip cookies. Then he started telling his weekly ghost story. "Once upon a time, there was an old man who lived in a house with his wife." Cousin Fred paused to scrutinize their attentiveness.

"Fearing that his beautiful wife would abandon him, he forbade her to leave the house. So she sat in front of the mirror all day, alone, talking to herself. Every day after work, the old man stopped at the neighborhood hardware store and bought a piece of glass to build a glass house for his wife so she could see the beautiful landscape. But before the glass house was completed, his wife died."

We moved about nervously and Cousin Fred paused before continuing. "After that, the old man always slept on his packed suitcase so he'd be ready to join his wife when the time came. Then one night, while he was trying to sleep, he heard a scratching sound on the glass." We too heard the noise … squeak squeak squeak … and we saw terror and alarming evil in Cousin Fred's eyes.

"After the old man heard the noise," Cousin Fred continued, "he sat up on his suitcase, wondering if the noise came from those damn neighborhood kids. Then he lay back down and eventually fell asleep."

Suddenly Cousin Fred rushed out of the room. When he came back, just a moment later, a creepy grin spread over his face and a stench filled the room. Then we heard someone banging on the front door, as if trying to break in. Cookies flew everywhere. Yelling and screaming incoherently, the children reached for their blankets to cover their heads.

Cousin Fred walked curiously but unhurriedly to the front door, and as he opened it stillness filled the room. "No one is at the door," he said.

He continued. "For years, the old man slept on his packed suitcase and waited to be united with his wife. One night, he sleepwalked, and he woke up the next day inside a casket at my funeral home. I asked the old man, 'What are you doing here?' The old man said, 'I don't know. I fell asleep in my house, but how did I end up here?' 'Well, I don't know,' I said. 'I didn't bring you here. If you're ready for your funeral I can accommodate you. But first I must check my schedule.'"

"As I turned to get my calendar, the old man yelled loudly from the casket, 'Wait, wait! Since I'm here, can you bring my wife back?' I told the old man that yes, I could wake the dead. The old man said, 'I'm not dead, but can you please bring my wife back?' I told him that when he died I would bring him and his wife back at the same time."

"I closed that old man's casket five years ago," Uncle Fred said in a matter-of-fact manner. "So tonight, I've invited him and his wife here to introduce them to you all."

As the front door and the windows slammed open and shut, the children heard two people enter from the back door of Cousin Fred's house.

Desperately, chaotically, wildly, everyone crashed out the front door.

"Ma! Ma! Ma!" Screaming hysterically, Honey Gal runs into Grandmother's house. "Johnnie is hurt!" Hazel calmly places the baby on the blanket as she rises from the floor. Aunt Juanita yells, "What happened?" She and Hazel follow Honey Gal outside into the moonless night to the bottom of hill, where Johnnie lies in a pool of blood, telling Ma she is sorry for hurting herself. Aunt Juanita and her son, Alto Jr., help carry Johnnie into the house. "Ma, I'm sorry. I told Johnnie not to ride fast on the bike while driving downhill," says Honey Gal. "I didn't know she was going to fall and hurt herself."

"Betty, shut up," says my cousin Pee Ann. "Why are you crying and screaming? Nothing is wrong with you." But I scream louder. Johnnie is my heart. My neck is hurting because they are having to hold a rag around her neck to stop the bleeding, and I think Johnnie is going to die. Aunt Juanita and Uncle Alto drive Ma and Johnnie to the doctor. I cry myself to sleep while Sarah comforts her back, sore from Ma's fist bruise.

Waking up the next morning and seeing Johnnie lying on a pallet next to me brings peace to my heart. I roll closer to investigate the large bandage around her neck. "Johnnie, can I get you something?" I ask. "You can move further away before you hurt my neck!" Then Honey Gal walks in, holding the baby, our sister Ann, and tells us to get up. We are going home.

MIGRANT WORKER

A huge, rumbling trailer truck, larger than our three-room house, is parked right up on our porch. It is barely dawn and the lights on the truck illuminate our path as we stumble out of bed, carrying our belongings inside pillowcases. The back of the truck is full of people. The grass is wet.

In 1956, the mill where my Dad worked burned down. The owner had no insurance and no money to have it rebuilt, so we became migrant workers, traveling according to the harvest seasons from Florida and Alabama up to New York. I was nine years old. Sarah was eighteen; Johnnie Mae, fifteen; Bush, thirteen; Melvin, seven; Sammy, five, and Ann, still in diapers. Now suddenly we all had to work to help support the family; my sister Bush and both my brothers quit elementary school so they could work.

It was our neighbor, Mrs. Johnnie Mae, who hooked Ma and Dad up with a migrant contractor. Mrs. Johnnie Mae was paid a fee for everyone she recruited. Later, when she noticed we had moved permanently from Troy, she also bought our house.

Early one morning we were loaded into an enclosed transfer truck, like cattle. We were the last to get on, and we had to scramble to find any room at all. There were probably eighteen adults and between seventy-five and ninety children. Each family had some eight to ten children; only families with a lot of kids were recruited. Everyone was sitting cross-legged because there was no room to stretch out, not even for the small children.

Throughout the long journey that ensued, every time I tried to stretch out and sleep, someone would stick what felt like a pin into me to keep me out of their space. Whenever I looked around to see who the culprit was, I never observed any guilty person. The children around me always had their heads down or pretended they were sleep. There was just no getting comfortable.

We were in the very rear of the truck, and there was nothing to hold us in. I was afraid we were going to fall out, especially when going up a steep hill. Whenever we crossed a bridge I was afraid we would fall into the water. And we were hungry the whole time. Ma was supposed to have been saving money for our trip, but now we found out there was no money, not even for food. We had to watch the people around us eating, and to entertain ourselves with the hungry sounds of our stomachs.

That journey turned our lives upside down. We had not traveled out of the city of Troy except for the one time when I had to have eye surgery. Every time we crossed a bridge it was like being hung in the air with nothing to catch us if we fell; that's how it seemed the rest of my life was going to be. It was like something had taken control. We had no power over what happened to us, just like we had no power over the sun sunning, or the moon setting.

After about four days, we finally reached Utica, New York. Then we traveled about fifty miles into the country, where we were unloaded at a kind of plantation. When the truck stopped, everyone tried to jump out at once, shuffling, yelling, shouting, pushing, and swearing. Several people were hurt, including elderly persons and parents who had to jump from the truck with their babies in their arms.

What we saw first was a huge two-story house, which looked abandoned; it looked like our witch's house except it had two levels instead of one. It was surrounded by dozens of two-room log cabins, joined together into several rows. The cabins shared a kitchen, an outhouse, a card room, and a kind of club house. This is where we would live.

Starting the next day, every child over six years old and all adults went to work picking beans. At nine years old I may have been the oldest person left in the camp. Overnight I went from being a cared-for child to being the babysitter of my three young siblings and a neighbor's infant.

The children were with me every day, from the time I got them up and dressed in the morning until the others came home at sundown. They came with me wherever I went, and I made sure they were clean and safe and fed. Our baby, Ann, and the neighbor's baby were still in diapers and had to be bottle fed. I also did the laundry and cleaned the cabin.

We children did have some time to play with each other. One migrant family we were friendly with was the Clims. They had traveled with us from Troy to Utica, and they had eight or nine children. Their boys were about my age, too young to work. So they were also around the camp during the day, and we'd go exploring together—travel through the swamp in back, run through the vacant building. Playing with them was just like playing with Aunt Juanita's boys, and Johnnie and Bush were friends with their older daughters. Mr. Clim's father, Roy Miles, was the seasonal contractor.

The endless swamp that extended in the back of the camp as far as anyone could see was one of our favorite haunts. Often, we and the Clim boys and any other children around would travel into the forest. It was part of our daily routine on those days when we were in camp alone for at least ten hours with nothing to do. Until one day we walked into a huge black bear walking upright, eating leaves from the trees. I experienced the exact type of fear that I'd experienced while fleeing Cousin Fred's house after listening to one of his ghost stories.

Soon enough, I figured out a way to make things more interesting; on weekends I became an entrepreneur to help put food on the table. This was my idea. First I staged dance contests as entertainment for the families. The young children would dance on a makeshift stage while the men in the audience threw pennies, nickels, and dimes at the children they thought should win.

After I got a little older, I started playing cards with the adults—mostly a game called pitty pat. The card club shack was closed to children, but I would press my ear against the door to hear what they were playing, and then I'd glide into the smoke-filled room as if I were one of the adults. Oddly enough, the men would welcome me into the game. Some older boys who had gotten the gambling bug would be there throwing away the little money their family had given them for their week's work, but I was always the only female child.

There was a woman there who served drinks. Four people at most could play the game. My turn always seemed to come when most of the players had gone home, broke and sad, like drunken sailors. I would be at the table with a few men with large families, who should have been ashamed to risk their weekly earnings. Each game was short: lasting from one minute to less than three minutes at most.

And I won—a lot. Most nights I left with so much cash I was too nervous to count it. I'd run to our cabin, looking back to make sure I wasn't robbed. I was at the peak of my game in self-defense, though, and would have raised holy hell if anybody had grabbed me. I'd rush into the house and give Ma my takings.

She never asked where I got the money, and she probably wouldn't have cared even if I had prostituted myself. Her motto was "Ask not what I can do for you. It's what you can do for me." So the thing was to just give it to her. Myself, I was just after the touch I received from her as she took the money out of my hands. Just that touch—so I could feel human, so I could know that this life was real.

Instead of going back to Alabama when the bean season was over, we followed the contractor, Mr. Miles, and moved to Belle Glade, Florida, a small farming community forty miles west of West Palm Beach, just outside the Everglades on the southern tip of Lake Okeechobee. About half of the sugarcane in the nation is grown in the mucklands there, and it is still home to a large population of Haitian, Jamaican, and American Black people. I did a lot of my growing up there.

After our first season in Belle Glade, Ma and most of us children went back to Utica, New York, to pick beans again. Honey Gal went to New York to stay with Dad's sister, and Dad stayed in Florida; he had found a year-around job stacking sod, and he was not interested in traveling up and down the road doing seasonal work.

Back in Utica, the Clims' children started giving us problems because they found out Ma was seeing their father, and they did not like their father cheating on their mother. It became war. "If you come out of that door, I'm going to beat your black ass, and pull all that nappy hair out of your head!" one of the Clim boys would yell. "Go to hell!" I'd scream. "And take your little stinking ass brother with you. Go and take a bath, because you stink!"

I couldn't beat up Mr. Clim's boys, but I knew how to get even with them. One day I would do something to them, and the next day they would do something to us. Once I covered the colored clothing hanging on their clothesline with a concoction of Clorox, ketchup, and mustard. They would usually just hit us with sticks; we'd run into our cabin and the

Clim kids would stand outside, calling us names and daring us to come out.

Some days I was afraid to leave the cabin for fear of getting beaten up. I would awaken to the sounds of bricks being thrown against the door. I'd peek out the crack in the door. One of the Clim boys would be standing there, peeking on our door step, daring us to come out. But I came out only when the adults returned from work.

Dad came to visit us in New York when he heard Ma was having an affair with Mr. Clim. Then, when the season was over in Utica, we all returned to Belle Glade. We were all living together there when Ma left Dad. It took some time. "Hazel, I know you are not going to the movie every time," Dad would say patiently. "Son!" she'd say. "I went to the movie. I've my ticket stub. Do you want to see it?" The room would quiet down and I'd go back to sleep. I heard that conversation many times before Ma decided to leave Dad.

Ma separated from Dad when she found out she was pregnant with Mr. Clim's child. She waited for Dad to leave for work one morning, and then she loaded us all in the car and we followed Mr. Clim back to Quincy, where he had already settled his family on a tobacco farm. All us children went with Ma except Johnnie, who stayed with Dad. He remained a broken man the rest of his life, a weekend alcoholic. Even as a child, I saw the pain in Dad's face and in his movement. When we were together, I tried to convince him that my new baby sister, Cookie, was his daughter and not Mr. Clim's. I knew it took a baby nine months inside the mother, but I didn't know how it got there; I thought you just had to live together. So over and over I would count the months and say to Dad, "Ma was here with you. The baby is yours." I was trying to make him feel better.

As for Mr. Clim, he visited our home often. During his weekend visits, he always fell asleep, probably after having too much to drink. He slept with his mouth open. One weekend, I made a sour concoction and poured it down his mouth. Of course, I got beat down. Ma never had to look far to find the culprit, and she didn't this time either. After he vomited up red, blue, and white stuff, complaining and coughing, she didn't have to look far. "Who put that stuff in Clim's mouth?" I heard her yell from the living room, as I locked myself inside the bedroom. "Who put that stuff in Clim's mouth?" I leaned my ear against the bedroom door, and the next thing I knew, I was being dragged by Bush to the living room by my legs, as Ma proceed to beat me with a stick. It hurt, but it wasn't surprising. Even if I denied doing something, my siblings never felt the need to defend me. They'd squeal on me in a second. And now that Johnnie wasn't there, Ma only had me to beat.

When Honey Gal returned from New York, she was responsible for us when Ma left the house. She had spent two years in Mobile, Alabama, living with my mother's brother, who sent her to business college to become a secretary. She then lived briefly in New York with our dad's sister Aunt Susie Mae before returning to live with us in Quincy, getting married, and moving back to Mobile. Talking about beautiful, that girl was tall! Yes, six feet tall: slim, built like a coca cola bottle. She had curves in all the right places, and long braids relaxed on her shoulder. I would stare at her because I couldn't believe how beautiful she was and that she was my sister. I had two beautiful people to brag about, Ma and Honey Gal.

Now Honey Gal would tell Ma whenever we didn't listen to her and if we did something she felt we shouldn't have. Now once she had told me that Ma hadn't wanted us sucking from a bottle after we were a year old. And there was Cookie, our sister by Mr. Clim, still walking around with a bottle, only

18

days away from three years old! So one day when Ma left, I took the milk out of Cookie's bottle and put water in it. When Ma found out who did it, she beat me mercilessly. Sometimes Honey Gal would beg Ma to stop beating me and beat her instead.

Now like I said, Ma had a way of beating the life out of you. It was more than abuse; it was torture. I think I could have with stood waterboarding better than the pain she inflicted upon me. Finally at some point during a beating, I'd feel no pain: my body had exhausted all the signals it could send to my brain to register the feeling. But Ma did not stop. Sometimes I wanted to run away after a beating. I'd go into the corn field and stay there all day. My heart yearned for someone to come and look for me. No one came. I'd lay on the dirt between the corn rows until I got tired, and then I'd get up and go home.

I was always looking for a way out, even if it was only a temporary escape. Once I attended a week-long revival meeting of a Pentecostal traveling ministry. I participated in the rituals, even going as far as sitting on the morning bench and waiting for the spirit of the Lord. It was the fifth day of the meeting—the ministry was scheduled to move on the next day—and still I was not feeling anything. So I stood up and pretended to move uncontrollably so they'd think I had received the Spirit. It didn't work. Or maybe it did—after that I did at least find pleasure.

Several months after we moved to Quincy, Johnnie came to visit us. She had a suitcase full of brand new clothing, a necklace, and a birthstone ring. The clothing didn't impress me at all, but I was excited to see that there was such a thing as a birthstone ring. I wanted one of them rings because it would represent me. So when summer was over, I went with Johnnie back to Belle Glade to stay with Dad. This was in

1958. He said he would send tickets to any of us children who wanted to stay with him.

Johnnie had always been my hero. Earlier, when we lived in Troy, she used her presence to state herself, to claim her rights, and I had admired that in her. But when we became migrant workers, her personality completely changed. I didn't notice it, but I guess it was because we were moved out of our element. In Alabama our world had been familiar: our place, Grandma's house, Auntie's house, school, church. Now we were always in different places, always surrounded by strangers.

When we got on that first truck in Troy, headed for Utica, we may have been the only family who had experienced a stable life. We were kind, docile people, while the others may have been living from hand to mouth all their lives. They were hardened and prepared for what lay ahead. I'm thinking of that kid next to me on the truck, sticking me with a pin for leaning on him while I was asleep. I had no way to respond to that.

Anyway, I never noticed the change, in Johnnie or in myself; I was too busy trying to deal with my new life. So I copied Johnnie's old way of walking, her fierce eye—staking my claim like a rooster in a hen house. I learned to love swearing, to use my mouth as a weapon with real power. I knew that if you could organize the words that had the most stabbing effect—"son of a bitch," "mother fucker"—then you had more power than those with physical ability.

At one point Dad allowed his co-worker Shorty to stay with us because he had no place to live. He didn't last long.

Early one quiet winter morning, I was sleeping on my back when a cool breeze on my shoulder gradually moved down to my waist and wakened me from sleep. I slitted my eyes open and saw Shorty, butt naked and muscular, slowly pulling the cover off me as he straddled my legs. I saw that with every breath I took, he was cautiously pulling the cover further and further. I nearly exploded with fear and absolute contempt. But I was onto him; I became stronger and more brave with each breath. As he pulled the covers, I would inhale, getting ready for what I would do. By the time he was ready to try to bear down on my chest, I threw my sturdy arms up against him and struck his balls with my right foot, pushing his muscular body off me. He was on the floor and I was sprinting to a neighbor's room, just two doors down the hall.

I told my Dad when he came home from work, and he told Shorty to move. "Shorty," he said, "Betty told me you got in the bed with her with no clothing on!"

"I ... I ..."

"Never mind answering. I want you to get all your things and get moved right now. You cannot stay here."

"Mr. Owens, I don't have no money and no place to stay!"

"Well! I helped you by allowing you to stay here, but you are not welcome in my home anymore."

And that was that.

When Johnnie was sixteen and in the eleventh grade, she got pregnant and dropped out of high school. There was a rumor that Johnnie and Dad were having sex. Much later, she confided in me that she may have had touched Dad inappropriately, and he told her, "Johnnie, I'm your Dad." I just listened and did not say a word. Out of the blue she just said it one day when we were in the car together. I never told anyone. But the rumor had been there. I also heard that it was Ma who started that rumor because she was jealous and angry because when she took all of us with her when she moved to Quincy, Johnnie refused to go. Either way, there it was. Johnnie was leaving.

Johnnie married her baby's daddy, Elijah, and they moved back with his family on a farm in his hometown in Mississippi. Elijah was abusive, and Johnnie found life horrible. While pregnant with her second child, she set herself on fire. Johnnie said to me, "Betty, I had not intended to kill myself. It was just a scream for help." She explained what happened. "One night, Elijah had gone out on his regularly weekend outing. I put kerosene on my skirt. The flame exploded over my dress; I couldn't put it out and I started screaming for help; Elijah's sister and mother threw a bucket of water to put the fire out."

She had severe burns on her thigh, hand, and stomach. Because she did not receive proper care for her wounds, she had obvious scars. The first thing that you'd notice about Johnnie was the scar on her hand. It looked like it had been half cooked in scorching oil. Skin was grafted from her thigh to replace the skin on her wrist, but since she did not receive proper care of the injury, it healed with layers of scar tissue.

But this was all later. At the time of her departure, I knew nothing of the rumors. I didn't know why she was leaving. All I knew was that I was already lonely without her. My heart felt empty. Like a young child, I didn't know how to express hurt and pain. All I knew was how to show anger. So when Johnnie told me she was getting married and leaving, I threw all her clothing from the balcony of the building.

Years later, when I expressed to Johnnie how hurt I had been when she left me and moved out of state, she said, "Betty, I thought you hated me. If I had known you didn't

22

want me to leave I wouldn't have left." If only I had known that. I had always been jealous of Elijah for her. Even before Johnnie got pregnant, when she was dating him, I tied her to the bed to prevent her from going out with him. "Elijah," I'd say, "why are you here?"

"I came to take Johnnie to the movies."

"She can't go to the movies," I'd say sternly.

"Well! I have three dollars I can give you to buy something from the second-hand store or go to the movies." And of course, I'd have to take the money. But I wasn't happy about her and Elijah. And when she was gone, I was devastated.

Even my Dad noticed something was wrong with me. We had gotten close living together, and I tried to help him with his own sorrow. While sitting on the porch late at night, I'd see my dad straggling home with only the shadows of his feet leading him back to our building. As he used the handrail to pull his body forward, he'd murmured to me, "Bebe, Hazel is a dirty woman."

"I understand, Dad." I'd say. "Let me take your hand and walk you to the door."

"No! Don't hold my hand. I'll walk myself."

"Okay, Dad. Good night."

Then Dad would either lie in front of the door or sometimes he would go inside or go to bed; it all depended upon the weather and his asthma condition. He was the walking wounded. Even as a child, my dad taught me how a broken heart looked. I'm sure that many nights he laid awake thinking that if they had never left Troy, he would still have his wife.

Although Dad was dealing with his own broken heart, he was aware of the pain I felt when Johnnie left me. I'm sure that was why he suggested that I go and live with Ma and my siblings. So the summer before the sixth grade, when I was twelve, I stayed with them in Quincy, where Ma had followed Mr. Clim and his family to work in tobacco fields. I rode eight hours on a hot Greyhound bus to get there. Although I stared out the window constantly so I would not miss my stop, I missed it by two miles. So I had to walk that distance.

As I got closer to Ma's cabin, the smell of fried fish came to meet me. I felt better and began to walk faster. I saw my nappy-haired brother Jab, obedient Sammy, and nurse Ann playing in the front yard with straw sticks. They looked at me, burdened down with two suitcases, and they continued to play.

Once inside the house, I threw my bags on the floor and grabbed a plate of food. Ma was having a fish party. Several men were there, including Mr. Clim. As I sat in a chair chowing down on the hot fish, I noticed a young man with soft brown eyes, about seventeen years old, staring at me. Before I could understand his attention, my sister Bush, who was around fourteen, came over, took me by the hand, and whispered that this was Jake, and that he had a girlfriend, who lived in the next cabin.

Jake was still staring at me when the girlfriend, Mary Bell, arrived at the party. I didn't know then that she was the girlfriend, but I sure found out the next day. Walking home from the store, I unknowingly passed by Mary Bell's house. She ran out into the road, her red skin blazing from pure violence. Hideous as a street thug, she said, "Jake is my boyfriend, and you better not talk to him." Before I could

24

register her comments and put her back in her place, she pulled out a butcher knife and stabbed me in the chest, near my heart. In less than a second, before the knife was removed from my chest, I started running home like an injured dog, hit by a car. I ran like a terrified deer as she sprinted behind me, like a tiger who has not eaten in several days. Once in arm's length of catching me, she reached forward and stabbed me in my left shoulder, branding it for life. If I had not run she probably would have killed me.

I ran home screaming loud, scared to death and hoping my family would come to my rescue. Bush waved down a car headed to town and told the driver to tell the police to come to our house. When the cops arrived, I was sitting in the house with a rag over my chest and shoulder to stop the bleeding. Instead of taking me to the doctor's office, the police officer took both Mary Beth—the red, blue-eyed girl with long straight hair—and me—dark brown, nappy haired, large lipped, and wide-nosed Betty—to the police department. I couldn't believe it. I told the police I was hurt and I did not start the fight. The cop said, "You shut up." He threatened to lock both of us up if we got into any more trouble. Think about the "scared straight" programs they use to deter troubled youth from committing crimes. Well, it worked for me.

At that point, I thought I was through with romance. I continued to go to the store for Ma every day during my stay, but I always anxiously scoped my surroundings and walked swiftly, especially while passing Mary Bell's house. When Jake heard what happened, he came to my mother's cabin and told me he was sorry. He said, "Mary Bell and I are not girlfriend and boyfriend anymore." I said, "I don't care. I'm not interested in dating."

But every night after work Jake came to our house. We sat on the porch and talked. He held my hand, touched my

25

ears and forehead, and tried to kiss me on the lips. He had yielding lips and silky, flawless skin. With each touch, my entire body exploded in ecstasy. But I forced my mind to force my hands to push him back. It was always "No! I have a handsome boyfriend who loves me." But all the time I was thinking, "Do you really want me? Why?"

After sitting on the porch for months, Jake and I started walking every evening down the red dirt road in front of our cabin. Many nights we walked that road, talking and holding hands. Whenever we turned to go home, before I knew what had happened, Jake had me pinned against the wall of the red clay dirt road, trying to force his penis between my legs. But all of us siblings inherited physical strength from both sides of the family. Even Bush, who had a blood problem, was as strong as a horse. When I was in my middle teens I could pick up a large tub of water. So even though Jake made several of these attempts to force himself on me, he was not successful. Then the tobacco season was over and we all moved back to Belle Glade.

Later, Jake and several of his friends moved to Belle Glade to work in the fields: packing corn or celery, picking beans, stacking sod. He continued to pursue me, and although he was irresistible, I never felt the need to allow him to have sex with me. I felt brave around him because he was never forceful and I knew he never could get inside me, regardless of how hard he tried. I didn't worry about him because after probably twenty tries he could never do it. And he never hit me.

Then on one occasion, we were lying on his floor in his room playing around. I had started giving him permission to rub his body against mine. I thought this night would be like any other night, but before I realized it, his penis was inside of me. I flew out of his room like a jet taking off a runway and ran home. The insertion frightened me, and after that incident, I never went to his room again, even though he tried to persuade me to continue seeing him. It scared me to death. We stopped seeing each other after that incident.

> *Your touch jolts my mind*
> *and I can feel it does the same to your*
> *spine.*
> *But what I want is to know*
> *what you see in me.*
> *My thick nappy hair, the nose that*
> *covers my face*
> *the large lips that won't stay closed?*
> *Your brown skin, sparkling eyes*
> *your body, carved in gold—*
> *Who wouldn't want this priceless*
> *statue?*
> *But what I want is to know*
> *what you see in me*

In Quincy we had a swing on the porch, and I liked to sit on the swing, even though there was nothing to see but wide opened space and cornfields as far as you could see. Usually my only form of entertainment while sitting on the porch was daydreaming and thinking. But that summer I was truly entertained when the chain gang workers began working on the dirt road in front of our cabin. I didn't feel afraid because several guards with weapons supervised them as they worked. The prisoners made the time pass by singing and making unusual sounds.

One day while sitting on the porch, I went inside the cabin and found a paper and pencil. While looking and listening to prisoners, I wrote the lyrics to a song: "That's the sound of the men working on the chain gang." In the back of True Story magazine I had read an advertisement from

Motown/Barry Gordy, soliciting lyrics. So I sent my chain gang lyrics, along with several other songs I had written. Motown responded, saying that I had to pay money, I think twenty-five dollars, to have my song set to music. Our entire family was probably living off that amount for the entire month. But I continued to send lyrics and received encouraging letters to continue.

Years later I found out that the song "Chain Gang," which I recognized as my own, was supposed to have been written by Sam Cooke and released in 1960, four years after we became migrant workers. He said it was inspired by a chance meeting with a chain gang on a highway. I think this is a lie, because I first heard that song on the radio only a short time after I wrote it and sent it in.

Even with Jake, I wasn't happy in Quincy. Every day I complained about everything. Especially the food. I had been spoiled living with Dad, where I could go to the corner store where he had credit and select anything I wanted to eat. But in Quincy there was a corn field in back of our log cabin, so Ma cooked creamy corn and rice every day. I fussed about eating neck bones every day, too. We always had Kool Aid to drink with our dinner, but I demanded and got a soda to drink. I worked in the tobacco field and felt that for my hard work I should at least have a soda. My siblings never complained about anything.

The tobacco work was piece work: you were paid according to how much work you did. After the tobacco leaves were harvested, they were individually hand-strung in pairs onto a stick to hang in the barn. The poles, each with about a hundred leaves, were placed in the curing house at different levels. I was one of the trusted workers who counted and bundled the sticks to give to the workers to sew.

When the tobacco season was over, Bush and I worked picking cotton. We traveled to the cotton field before dawn on the back of a truck. Ma prepared food for us to take with us—usually a sandwich. Bush was always hungry, and I had to motivate her to keep working.

"Betty, when are we going to stop and eat lunch?"

"As soon as you fill that cotton bag, we can stop to eat, but until then, you will not get anything to eat."

I kept the lunch. Most days, Bush put forth her best effort, but she never acquired the stamina needed for field work. I worked really hard because the harder you worked, the more cotton you picked, and the more cotton you picked, the more money you earned. And I wanted to please Ma by showing my worth, and I knew we needed the money.

The work made me miss half the school days, and each night I prayed I would be promoted. I guess I was. But I don't remember school, either in Troy or in Quincy. I know I attended school in Troy until we migrated to Utica, and then I attended off and on in Quincy. And I know that when I started school in Troy, I already knew how to read and write because my older sisters had taught me.

My only specific memory about school at this time is being in a classroom and getting beat down on my hand with a ruler for talking out of turn and yelling out an answer when the teacher had asked another student the question. The classes at that school were taught all together, like a one-room schoolhouse. It was boring, so I was a rebel talking, which distracted the teacher from what she was doing. It may have even made her have to start the assignment over, and she did not like that. So she hit me. The licks were painful and my eyes watered, but not a tear rolled down my cheeks. Still, I think the beating destroyed my memory.

29

From Quincy we moved back to Belle Glade, where we stayed with Ma in an apartment building that rented rooms. (You see, migrant workers who followed the seasons had to give up their apartments each time they left for a new job, find a new residence in the new place, and repeat this process every season.) We shared one and a half rooms. The Clims moved back there, too. Our building, James Oliver's apartment building, had a second-hand store on the ground floor, and six apartments like ours on the second floor, three on each side of a central hallway. There was a front entrance and a back exit from the second floor. Everyone shared one bathroom near the exit of the building. Johnnie and her husband had moved back too, and she lived in an apartment across the hall from us. Dad was living up the street.

There was a time when every Saturday morning Dad would stand outside our apartment, in the middle of the street, calling Ma names before any of the neighbors were even up. His favorite thing to say was, "Hazel, you're a dirty woman." It was like Stanley yelling to Stella. Then he'd call his children down and give us our weekly allowance. Ma didn't mind that, but she did not want her business in the street. When the rant lasted longer than Ma could tolerate, she'd threaten to call the police on him; then he went home. This all lay like a cut on my heart.

One night while sound asleep, I was awakened by a noise coming from the back room where Ma slept, which doubled as the kitchen. It was Ma and Mr. Clim moaning and crooning while they were having sex. I started to cry, and Ma heard me. Ma said, "You cannot run my life. You get out of here and go and stay with your dad." I was kicked out of the room.

Crying hysterically, I tried to take shelter with Johnnie, across the hall. But Ma followed me and forced me out of the room. I went and sat on the top of the exit steps. Ma kicked me in my back as I went down all twenty steps, weeping soundlessly because I was too embarrassed for anyone to see I was being kicked and thrown out of the house. I was not feeling rejected; that I was used to. But I was overcome with confusion and shame, afraid that I would wake the neighbors. I finally stood up and walked to my dad's apartment. My dad took me in.

After Ma kicked me out of her house, I ceased to feel anything toward her. Those kicks gave me a wooden heart and started me on a journey of feeling only pain and pleasure, happy or sad—that's it. No in-between. No love. No hate. No contentment. No just feeling good. Just pain, and pleasure.

Only skilled laborers—like those who stack celery or corn, sugarcane cutters, packing house workers, drivers, or sod workers—had a steady job during the season. Everyone else was day labor. My Dad, for instance, was a sod worker on a sow ranch, and it was a steady job. The scorching Florida sunshine and the muck he worked in, which he was allergic to, had burned his black skin to a crispy dark black-gray, the same color as black gold, which was what they called the rich soil in the Everglades. His skin looked like alligator skin, like he had fish scales. Dad also had severe asthma. During most of his attacks, he lay on the cement floor in front of his room, and sometimes he lay on the cement floor on the other side of the balcony. During his episodes, I wondered what would happen to me if he died.

But at least he had work. It was piecework, which means he was paid according to how many pallets he stacked. With precision and accuracy, like an artist, he would stack pieces of grass, sixteen by sixteen, four feet wide and six feet high. The work was harsh, with constant stooping and reaching and twisting to stack the sod in scorching, blazing heat, which in the summer often exceeded 100 degrees.

If you were a day laborer, like most people, things were harder because finding work was a constant task. But I didn't mind. Once I moved in with Dad, I started focusing more on getting what I wanted, which at the time was spending money. So I picked beans every weekend to supplement the two dollars in weekly allowance I received from my dad.

If you wanted to work, you appeared at the loading ramp between four and five am. About the size of a city block, the loading ramp was where the trucks or buses backed up, waiting for workers. Each contractor would place down a sample of the work that would be done, and then they would perform like salesmen, advertising their products by telling workers how much they could earn. All the workers moved swiftly but meticulously from truck to truck, deciding which contractor they would work for.

Once you decided on the product you wanted to work, you lined up in front of the right truck or bus, ready to go. You tensed up. It was like the running of the bull that happens in Spain every year. When the horn blew at six o'clock, any line that had formed became obsolete, and if you didn't move fast enough, you could be trampled. Most of the time, the trucks or buses became full so fast that in a few minutes those who didn't find a spot would be running around in circles, trying to find spare space on any of the work transports. Imagine a Black Friday shopping spree and triple it—that's what it was like at the loading ramp for day workers when the whistle blew to get on the transport.

The work day was long and drudging. On most days we returned back to Belle Glade barely before dark. I usually earned about eight or ten dollars per day picking beans and spent about half of that on lunch food before I left the field. I spent the rest of the money on used clothing for school and for movies on the weekends. There was only one theater in town, and it played the same movie for weeks at a time. I lived for those weekend movies, and spending time with my friends Shirley and Barbara.

I knew we were poor; we were all poor. But I tried to find ways to inch up the ladder. For instance, I tried to get people to think that I was an only child. I wanted people to think that at least I had that going for me. Pretending to be an only child made me feel special, like it elevated me from being poor. Plus I felt better off than most people because my dad had steady work, and I could go to the corner store where he had credit and select anything I wanted to eat. But then one day, the school gave us a survey to complete, with questions like, do you share the bathroom with anyone other than your family? How many people live in your home? Do you share your bed with anyone else or how many people live in your room?

Those questions made me come to terms with how poor we were. They belittled me. I'd been able to shell our condition, but those questions made me realize that people living like us were destitute. The survey slapped me right in the face. In other words, it awakened me to my condition and made me realize that people were not supposed to live in those types of conditions. Up until then I thought I was better than the rest of the people. The survey showed me that I was just like them.

I did have the luck of the draw in ways that other people didn't, though. Take my neighbor and friend Christina, who lived in the two-room apartment adjoining ours. Christina was a couple years younger than me, but I enjoyed her company. One thing we had in common was that we both lived with our dads. When she moved in with her dad, she was around eleven or twelve and pregnant with a child.

33

When she had the baby girl, she named her after me and the baby's daddy: Betty Joe. I felt so honored. I often kept Betty Joe at night while Christina went out, until Dad stopped me from babysitting.

Later Christina moved out of her dad's apartment into her own room. On weekends, I would visit her and watch her dress up like an adult whore. Christina knew how to advertise her assets. She was about five feet tall and weighed about ninety pounds, maybe even less. She was bow-legged, which made her look even more appealing, and she was light skinned, and so there was no color she couldn't wear. She loved beautiful, silky, glittering outfits, and she was an expert at selecting the right clothing, makeup, and wigs, like short dresses or skirts to show off those carved bow legs and belts to show off her tiny waist and accent her small hips and butt. She wore long colorful wigs, and she put on makeup like an expert. She dressed like she was going to perform in a cabaret. Sometimes, she would fix me up with a wigs and makeup. I admired the glamour, but I took the makeup off before I went back home.

One day Christina confided in me that one of the city council members took her and several other young teens to the Jamaica camp. This was a barracks near Belle Glade that housed "guest workers" who were brought in from the Caribbean to cut sugar cane. Christina and the others were brought there to have sex with the men, who would line up in front of the doorway to take their turn. She may have received two to three dollars per sex partner, after the pimp got his share.

I feel fortunate that none of my acquaintances ever invited me to participate in that underworld, or draw me into doing anything illegal or becoming promiscuous. Usually they kept it a secret. And I had no desire to prostitute myself for the things I didn't have. I didn't want things; I wanted out.

Back after Johnnie got married and left Belle Glade, Dad and I had moved in with Ms. Easter. Ms. Easter was my Dad's sometimes sane housemate. She had been a professional housekeeper and cook, and she called my dad "Mr. Owens" and kept a superb house. She ironed the sheets for our beds and even ironed Dad's underwear. Basically, anything that could be washed and cleaned, she ironed.

I disliked everything about her. I showed this by removing the nicely pressed, white, clean-smelling sheets from my bed and sleeping on the mattress. Other times, I'd sleep on the floor. When she prepared a school lunch for me, I would refuse to take it. Anything she did to make herself feel worthy, I undid to make her feel bad. And my dad seemed to understand. He was patient with both of us.

"Mr. Owens, tell Betty to take the lunch I fixed her for school."

"Easter, don't worry. Just let Betty get something from the store. I've given her money for lunch."

"I don't see why you allow her to go to the store or give her money for lunch when she can take lunch with her!"

"Okay, Easter. It's okay."

Once Ma had kicked me out and I had returned to living with Dad, I had to contend with Ms. Easter again. Although my dad always showed me love by unconditionally taking care of me, providing food, clothing, and shelter, I took him for granted and did very little to help out. I figured I wasn't going to become a maid or a professional dishwasher, so why learn how to do household chores?

Plus, there was Ms. Easter to do everything. When Dad came home from work, she always had his crisply ironed clothing laid out for him on the bed, including underwear and tee shirt. He came home covered in the muck that he was allergic to, so the minute he arrived home he took a shower in our shared bathroom, which was also used by six other families in the apartment building. Then he could enjoy the balanced, eloquently prepared dinner that Ms. Easter had prepared on our two-eye hot plate. She placed the dinner on the kitchen table with what passed for decorum: with napkin, fork, spoon, and a glass of buttermilk. After dinner, depending on the weather, Dad would either sit on the porch in front of our front room or relax in his chair in the front room, which doubled as his and Ms. Easter's bedroom. My room doubled as the kitchen; with the hot plate, refrigerator, kitchen table with two chairs, a small wooden pantry, and my regular side bed.

Eventually my sister Ann, my dad's baby girl, moved in with us. She was about six years old at the time, she became the child Ms. Easter never had. Ms. Easter spent the allowance that Dad gave her on Ann.

When she first arrived, Ann was a mess. She had not been attending school on a regular basis because she had no one to take her. Ann's hair was matty because no one had been taking care of it. Her skin was covered in layers of dirt. So Ms. Easter scrubbed Ann's body daily, and every week Ann was sent to the beauty shop. Within a week, that girl's color changed: it became smooth and silky. Her hair shined like new money. I can't remember feeling any jealousy toward Ann; I didn't have to compete with her for Ms. Easter's attention because no attention was given or available to me. And since I did not particularly care about Ms. Easter, it didn't matter what she did for Ann.

Ms. Easter saw to it that Ann did her homework every day, and before she was put to bed at night, I would read her a bedtime story. With only a few books available, I started going to the back door of the public library to try and check out books. I was not allowed a library card, because black people were not supposed to use the library. But the librarian made arrangements for me to check out one book at a time and return it at the end of the week. When I returned the book, I would receive another book. Soon Ann was making straight As in school. My brothers and sisters started calling her "Tops."

After a few months of daily bedtime stories, she would not go to sleep unless I read her a story, and story time with Ann really interfered with my movie schedule. So I took her to the movies with me until Ms. Easter and Dad stopped me. Then Ann started sneaking out of the back door and walking to the corner of Fifth Street looking for me to come home from the movie and read her a story. Before that became a problem, Ma had Ann move back home with her to be a companion for Cookie, our younger sister by Mr. Clim.

Ms. Easter became so depressed when Ann left that she had a nervous breakdown and had to be hospitalized. After that, Dad and I started looking for the various abnormal activities that were typical for her before he called the mental institution to have her committed: she would start sitting on the porch half naked, with her private parts exposed; she'd start to walk the streets, talking to herself; she'd start using the wrong ingredients to cook a dish, like using cornmeal to make biscuits instead of flour. She'd mix the food in with various inedible concoctions, like I had fixed to put in Mr. Clim's mouth when he was drunk.

Usually Dad would allow Ms. Easter to stay home even with the unusual antics until the neighbors started to complain, and then he would have the hospital come and get her. And she would not leave without a fight. It was not easy getting a 300-pound woman down ten to twelve steps into an ambulance without the use of medication. The paramedics had trouble putting restraining equipment on her. She fought every step of the way, yelling incoherent obscenities throughout the ordeal.

Whenever she became ill, Ms. Easter openly showed her dislike for me, claiming that I was ill-mannered and disrespectful to her. Although I never talked back or showed any obvious contempt toward her, she knew that I didn't like her to be with my dad because I wanted him all to myself.

Sometimes I woke up at night to find Ms. Easter standing over me with a cast-iron skillet, threatening to hit me with it. I'd yell out loud, "Dad, Ms. Easter is standing over me with the cast-iron in a raised position like she's going to smash me with it!" Dad would say, "Easter, come out of that room and leave Betty alone." She'd leave my room and return to their bedroom and go to bed. Usually, I went back to sleep, but I made sure I slept next to the wall, where it was difficult for her to reach me without waking me up. Being next to the wall, I had to contend with huge flying roaches that shared the room with me and came out at night looking for food. When I tried to attack them, they just flew to a different part of the room. Anyway, that skillet was the limit, and the next day my Dad called the hospital for them to come and get Ms. Easter.

In the evenings I would sit on the side porch, watching life go by. The view was like a canvas that showed the life of our neighborhood, with pictures and my imagination to entertain me. Occasionally, a neighborhood friend would sit with me and give me the current updates on who's dating who and who's pregnant and by whom.

Everything became a part of my terrain while sitting those lonesome nights on the porch. As the darkness came on, I'd hear laughter, and cries, music from a neighbor's apartment or the nearest junk joint, shouts of triumph. On wintry nights when the wind blew, the fragrance of smoke from someone's outside barbecue pit business calmed my hunger.

Few people pass as I sit here. The man who lives next to us arrives home from work, his footsteps coming up the concrete steps and his lunch pail sliding on the rail as he limps to his front door. The music plays in the junk joint downstairs. A slender young man—balding, with holey black pants and a blue shirt with a white collar—darts into the alley, carrying something in a paper bag. Peeking from behind the building, he unzips his pants and begins to urinate against the wall. As he zips his pants, a middle-aged man with a wide-brimmed hat and studs on his shoes walks up to him. They hug and walk to the next corner, where they disappear.

For a moment, I leave this scene and conjure a scene the precise opposite. I don't know enough to dream up a nice neighborhood or a white picket fence; I just dream of freedom, being out of Belle Glade, anywhere but here.

But soon, all too soon, the unmistakable, dusty odor of muck returns. I am trapped.

INTENT TO ESCAPE

I am the only one of my siblings attending school. School is my life, my only enjoyment. The rest of the time I am sad, and I dread when the bell rings to go home. With no TV, radio, or homework, I spend my evenings sitting on the porch, watching the neighbors and contemplating a better life for myself.

The male neighbor who sits with me on the porch always uses explicit words to describe who's having sex with whom and who is pregnant. My body tingles from his description.

Like I said, every weekend I worked picking beans. With my earnings, I'd buy something at the second-hand store to wear to the movies and school. Every weekend, I went to the movies alone. My friend Shirley and I were in the tenth grade and our friend Barbara was in the ninth grade. Everyone called us the Three Stooges because we were always together on weekends.

Shirley and Barbara did not work in the fields, and they weren't allowed to go to the movies or even to go near 5th Street, where the juke joints and bars lined the street. Our building was on 6th Street, so I had to walk up only one block to get where all the adult action took place and where the movie theater was. But kids who lived in houses were too good to be in that area. Barbara's and Shirley's parents owned their own homes, in the best part of town. They lived about two to three houses apart from each other on the same street. People who lived there owned their own businesses or were teachers, principals, funeral home directors, or farm work contractors. Barbara's mother was a beautician, and her dad was a janitor at school. Shirley's parents had steady work, not seasonal. On weekends Shirley and I hung out at Barbara's mother's beauty salon while Barbara helped her mother with the customers. Otherwise, neither Barbara nor Shirley was seen in my neighborhood during the week days.

You wouldn't think so in a predominantly African American town, but even Belle Glade had a pecking order, or class code. There was a color line, but not like other parts of the country. At school it went like this: If your parents were teachers or owned their own business, you topped the list. If your parents didn't work in the fields and they owned their own home, you were next. If you lived in a house, you were next. If you lived in a room or an apartment and your parents worked in the fields, you were at the bottom of the line with the other migrant workers. Anything was better than working in the fields.

Your color shade played a role, too, but it wasn't as major as class and talent. If you were dark and really smart, you had game. You had more pull than your light or high yellow classmates. In high school, our leading majorette was dark skinned; she could out-swirl anyone else and was an honor student.

After Barbara's mother's shop closed, Barbara, Shirley Ann, and I would go hang out with Barbara's boyfriend in South Bay, which was about four miles from Belle Glade. We three would pretend that we were the Supremes and would harmonize. We'd stand on the street, talking and singing for hours. Barbara and her boyfriend would disappear to his room and return looking innocent. I never knew if they were actually having sex. We never discussed sex. When someone got pregnant, we talked about them, but never what it was the result of. Or maybe Shirley Ann and Barbara didn't discuss it around me.

It has always been my experience, except for Christina, that when you're doing something, you don't tell Betty. People always want me to think highly of them. Shirley Ann wanted me to think she was a virgin. I believed her until years later, when an ex-boyfriend of hers told me she came to his home every morning before school for sex. And it's true that Shirley was a seasonal girl in high school; whoever was the school's sports star was her boyfriend. When it was football, she dated the quarterback or the unstoppable running back; for basketball, it was the point guard or the person who scored the most points.

When I was in my middle teens, fourteen or fifteen, I joined Barbara's Holiness church. I got baptized. After joining the church, I joined the church choir. I also sang in the school choir. I was asked several times to be the lead in a song, but I was too shy and didn't have the confidence to step up to the plate at church. Barbara always led the songs, and she had an awesome voice.

In the school choir, we were separated into sections according to our voice range; I was in the alto section. We altos would practice our lines, and then the sopranos practiced theirs. But when it was time for both groups to sing together, I would sing soprano, which made the choir teacher crazy because she didn't know why a soprano pitch was coming from the alto section. I thought it was funny, but I never let on that it was me. Shirley was also in the choir, but she couldn't sing. I guess that's why we never tried to form a group. Shirley was our leader. She was good at pretending.

In the tenth grade, Mrs. Turner was my mathematics teacher. She was young and attractive, high yellow and very professional. I was a pudgy, dark teenager with nappy hair who dressed like I had raided a dumpster, with the strength of a tiger. Yet she took me under her wing, and her attention elevated my self-esteem to where I started figuring out how to escape this poverty-stricken town.

I was exceptionally smart in math, and I helped her teach the class. Sometimes I thought I could become a mathematician and work at the Kennedy Space Center. But the highest level of math taught at our school was fractions and percentages. So years later, when I enrolled in college calculus, still thinking I was all brilliant in math, I couldn't do a single problem because I had never even heard of pre-algebra, much less pre-calculus or trigonometry.

As an elective, I took typing. The typing teacher and Mrs. Turner were roommates. Mrs. Turner invited me over to their apartment and I received additional help with typing and shorthand from her roommate. I borrowed a typewriter from my neighbor, Pop, and eventually I got up to about fifty-five words per minute on a manual typewriter. I received a typing certificate for being the most skilled typist.

I never questioned why Mrs. Turner took to me; I just enjoyed the accolades. I was called the teacher's pet. She even took me home with her to Birmingham to visit her family during the Christmas break. Before we left for Alabama, she took me to a huge department store in West Palm Beach and told me to select what I wanted. I selected an umbrella, with which I planned to be swept away from Belle Glade during the next hurricane, like Mary Poppins. Mrs. Turner also purchased my first brand-new underwear and bra. I was so taken by the gifts, I was afraid to open the bag. She had to take them out and give them to me.

On our drive to Birmingham, we stopped in Troy, Alabama, at my Aunt Juanita's house. Were they surprised to see me with this young lady who looked like beauty queen!

When we arrived at her parent's mansion, she rang the doorbell and the door opened itself. I was astonished; how did that happen? Later, I learned we were buzzed in by the electronic door opener. Mrs. Turner's family showered me with gifts and allowed me to select what I wanted out of their grocery store. That didn't impress me too much, because I was accustomed to selecting what I wanted out of Meeks' store in our neighborhood, where Dad had a credit. The thing that did impress me was quite simple: at night Mrs. Turner entered my room and put an extra blanket on my bed. She tucked me in warmly while I lay quietly, pretending to sleep. To me that represented love, which was something that I was not accustomed to.

When we returned to Belle Glade, Mrs. Turner gave me one of her mink-looking coats, in which I paraded around school. I was not invisible anymore.

By the time I was in the tenth grade, my friend Barbara was dating a young man who lived in South Bay. So on Saturday nights when the beauty shop closed, Barbara, Shirley, and I started going to South Bay to hang out with him. Barbara's boyfriend had a friend named Ben Harden, who was a senior at our high school. Ben was a light shade of brown, about five foot nine, and of medium build with an athletic body. He was clean cut, with an expression like he wouldn't harm a fly, and a unique straight-standing posture, military style. He was preppy looking, his school attire being starch-ironed trousers and some variation of long-sleeve colored church shirt with a sweater. I liked Ben, but the few times I saw him in school, he never acknowledged me.

Now I was not in the business of having sex, but during these outings somehow I always ended up in Barbara's boyfriend's room with Ben, where he raped me. I never told anyone. This happened several times, until I stopped going to South Bay with Shirley and Barbara.

Then Ben started stalking me at my home, while I was sitting on the porch in the evening. He started sneaking up on me and coaxing me into walking him to the end of Avenue E, which was near our high school and several blocks from my home. Then he started encouraging me to walk with him to the next block, then the next block, then the intersection in front of the school. When I refused to walk with him, he twisted one of my arms in a painful hold behind my back and motioned to me to continue walking.

Although we passed several people sitting in front of their apartments, talking and cooling off from the hot weather, I didn't ask anyone for help. Instead, I coaxed Ben into letting me walk freely, and then took off in a run for my life. He caught me and raped me in an isolated area behind the school.

This happened several times, mostly late at night when very few people were on the street and it was pitch dark. It became eerily familiar. As Ben led me to the back of the high school, on my way to the gallows, we'd pass people on the street. "Ben, you're holding my hand too tight. Can you let me walk without twisting my arm behind my back? Can you let me walk by myself?"

"No! If I turn you loose you'll run!"

"I won't run! Just let me walk on my own!"

Sometimes I talked him into letting me walk free: then the second he released his grip on my arm, I'd take off like an injured dog. I'd take off for a run and he'd savagely run me down. It froze my soul. When we walked to the back of the school house, he stood in front of me, staring in my face. I didn't move, not even a flinch. He'd say, "Lay down!" If I hesitated or was slow to respond to his command, he'd punch me so hard that the next thing I'd remember he was him on top of me. I never tried to communicate with him to stop, not even a scream. It usually was over as fast as he started. The only communication was me begging him to let

45

me walk freely. I knew I was trapped. The only freedom was the escape.

After raping me he'd leave me there on the wet grass, as if nothing had happened. I don't remember him saying anything after he finished. He just got up and left me laying there. I don't remember crying, only sobbing as despair overcame me. I'd put on my wet, torn clothing to hide my nakedness and walked home through the back streets so no one would see me. I'd sneak through the back screen door of our apartment like an injured animal, as silent as the morning moon.

After several such sneak attacks, I still sat on the porch, but I would scan my surroundings as if I were in a war zone. When I saw Ben coming, I ran swiftly into my room. If he happened to capture me on the porch, I refused to leave regardless of the pain he used to twist my arms behind my back. Then I would scream, fighting him back for trying to twist my arm behind my back, grabbing his hand as he tried to punch me with a closed fist, and holding onto the balcony rail with all my strength as he tried to force me loose. Regardless of what he did, I didn't turn loose of that rail.

On one occasion, when he was getting the best of me by forcefully pulling my hand from the grip I had on the rail, I noticed a male stranger looking up at us trying to figure out what was going on. Before I knew it, I yelled to him below in the street, "Can you help me?" The stranger yelled, "What are you doing to her?"

Ben didn't say anything but ran down the stairs and disappeared into darkness. I guess I had learned the hard way what people now know: not to allow an attacker to take you to another place. Knowing what to allow and what not to allow is a difficult business when life is something that happens to you.

Once I told Ben that I was going to report him to the police or the school principal. He laughed in my face: "Who is going to believe you? No one will believe that I would be caught dead with someone like you. Look at you. No way would I be with someone ugly and poor and destitute like you, let alone rape them. Look at you!" I guess I believed what he said because the thought of telling anyone never crossed my mind again.

By this time I had already experienced being beaten at school by the principal because a male student told him I had cursed him out. The principal didn't need any witnesses. He took the male student's word and summoned me to the office, where he had me to lay across a chair. He took out his belt and hit me three hard licks. I shed not one tear. I was just a poor migrant worker against a model student.

I didn't tell anyone about Ben for many years. Some kids never tell. They conclude that they have done something wrong. In my case, Ben was different from Shorty, different from Jake. I didn't want it, but I didn't stop it. It happened. And I thought I caused it to happen. In that case, to tell is like telling on yourself. Everyone would know your secret, and you are ashamed of what happened. The shame you feel is more profound that the anger you could ever feel in telling. Telling will not lessen the pain. And besides, who would believe you?

Maybe that is why you don't tell, because telling will not erase what has happened to you. Telling will not replace what has been lost; it will only add more shame. So it becomes your secret, and it embeds itself in your conscious and subconscious life for as long as you inhale and exhale. It deprives you of the intimate and emotional pleasure the Lord has made. It takes away a part of self.

During the summer of 1965, it seemed like the entire population had left the poverty-scarred town of Belle Glade and followed the growing season. Even the huge population of contracted Jamaicans and Haitians returned to their home countries during the summer.

The newspaper man who walked the streets in the early morning, yelling a tragedy from block to block to sell his papers ("Sonny Boy got his head cut off")—even he was no longer around. Nothing was the same—there was no sign of the usual. The moon had packed up and left, and each night was pitch dark except for the light from the few street lights, which was not even enough to see your feet in front of you as you walked. Even the wind had stopped blowing. Several folks mentioned that they saw a rat, cat, and dog standing on the corner with their thumbs out trying to hitch a ride out of town.

Even the mother and daughter who lived in the apartment across the street had disappeared. Usually, when nothing else was going on in the streets, I could count on this mother and daughter for entertainment. Watching them was like watching reality TV. They didn't hang their dirty laundry outside, but everyone knew what they were doing to earn a living.

The two women lived in an apartment that had two bedrooms, a kitchen, and a private bathroom. They even had colored light bulbs. I saw both black and white businessmen coming and going throughout the night, pretending they were "insurance men." I wondered where the women were getting the money to buy insurance from, because they never left their home to get to work. Yet they were among the very few in town who could afford a brand new car every year and had an air conditioner in their front and back doors.

But what choice did they have? They had to pay their rent and buy food. What choices did any of us have?

As for me, I was going into the twelfth grade in the fall. Ben had stopped raping me. I had survived for over a year without having anyone physically or mentally abuse me. And I had started riding at night with Joe, Christina, and Fred.

Who in town wouldn't die for a date with Fred?

Christina had told me that her boyfriend's friend Fred wanted to meet me and wanted me to go riding with them. Initially, I wasn't interested in riding with them, but Christina's persuasion assured me that it was okay. She would be in the car and nothing was going to happen to me. And I trusted Christina. So one night, after they had tried to get me to ride in the car for months without any success, Joe pulled over to the curb and Christina came up the stairs and told me Fred wanted to meet me. And I agreed.

Fred was a dropout, but every woman in town wanted a piece of him (and he tried hard to please them all). Tall, thin, brown skinned, eye color noticeably lighter than most black folks' eyes. And handsome! He would have been voted the most popular street person in Belle Glade, and he definitely would have topped the pecking order list. As a dancer, he could have competed with Michael Jackson's dual moves. When he was on the dance floor, people stopped dancing to look at him.

What's more, Fred appeared modest. That was part of his allure. He wasn't conceited. He was pigeon toed, with slightly bowed legs. An outstanding pool player, he had what people call "swagger." He was It! Like Denzel Washington. He had a love church, and I got baptized. The moment I gave into his interest in me, I became addicted to it. His interest in me made me feel like I was someone, like I was alive.

49

Fred's best friend was Joe Benjamin, and Joe's dad, Mr. Benjamin, was the manager of one of the most popular bars in Belle Glade. And after working hard all week in back-breaking conditions, in the scorching hot, humid heat, the town lived for the weekend.

As I stood on the corner of 5th Street, I had a bird's-eye view of women and men going from bar to bar, laughing, holding hands, with their Sunday best on. Well, not their Sunday best—their Saturday night best: short, hip-hugging skirts and colorful blouses. It was the place to be. Just watching people, you felt a part of the festival. The latest songs bounced off the walls of the buildings as the music spilled into the street. The music, alcohol, and a companion on their arms appeared to have given everyone a sense of utopia. The people of Belle Glade lived for the weekend; it was when they emerged from their despair into the consciousness of hope and fulfillment, with alcohol, music, and dance to ease the pain.

So Mr. Benjamin was worshipped and admired by everyone, including the other entrepreneurs in town. Since Joe and Fred were inseparable friends, Joe shared his toys with Fred. Joe's dad had several new model cars, so Fred got to drive the cars around town. He drove them as if they were his.

Driving a car gave you more status than owning a home, even if the car wasn't yours. Just driving a car drew attention to you. With a car you could go from a nobody to a somebody. Like when one of our high school graduates got a job folding clothing at a laundry. All the migrant workers were envious of her because she drove around in the owner's white van while picking up and delivering laundry.

Joe was Christina's boyfriend and the father of her baby girl, Betty Joe. When I first started riding with them, Joe drove, Christina sat in the front, and Fred and I sat in the back. We rode around the deserted town in a different car every night. Although I was hesitant about being in the car with them, I knew Christina was not going to let anything happen to me against my will.

But every night, there was less and less room in the back seat. Fred moved closer and closer to me, and soon I would have fallen out of the car if someone had said "Boo." Then he started holding my hand: "Betty, may I hold your hand?" he said kindly. I nodded and shyly said "yes." During our next outing, he asked again, "May I hold your hand?" And then, "May I put my arm around your shoulder?"

So this process continued until I allowed him to put his hand on my leg. Then he tried to kiss me on the lips. This continued for months. He held my hand; held my hand and put his arm around my shoulder; held my hand, put his arm around my shoulder, and put his hand on my thigh; held my hand, put his arm around my shoulder, put his hand on my thigh, and kissed me ...

Eventually Fred and I were riding in the car alone. We had sex in various cars all over that empty town, in every back alley, in all the isolated fields in the area. Eventually, we started having sex in the back room of his sister's house. Normally he picked me up while I was sitting on the porch, late at night, but when school started and I went to bed earlier, I would hear a light scratch at the back screen door late at night, like a robot hooked up to a door scratch, an alarm clock. I'd sneak out of the back door and dissolve into the cool windy night with Fred.

It was easy for me to like Fred, because he never tried to force himself on me and he wanted to be with me.

By wintertime, I noticed that the smell of food from the school cafeteria was making me sick to my stomach. Then I noticed that I had to urinate more often than usual in between classes. I didn't know what was going on. Then while eating lunch at school one day, I had to rush to the bathroom because I didn't want to vomit on the floor. One of my classmates said, "Are you pregnant?"

"Of course, I'm not pregnant," I said angrily. We were always on the watch out for pregnant girls in our school. It seem like they dropped out before they even started showing. But I knew something was wrong. I was pregnant. (Ironically, by that January health workers were canvassing the neighborhood, passing out birth control pills. How different my life might have been if only they had come a few months earlier!)

One night Fred and I were the back of a car in the swamp. Fred was removing my underwear. All of a sudden I blurted out that he had done enough damage, because I was pregnant. He smirked with a spark of excitement, but before he could proceed to celebrate, I begged him not to tell anyone because I would be thrown out of school for being pregnant, and I wanted to graduate. But it seemed that before I even got home that night, Fred had advertised to the entire town that he was expecting a baby and that "virgin Betty" was the mother of his child.

I continued my nightly escapades with Fred, and I continued to attend school. I used various wardrobe malfunctions to conceal my pregnancy. But right before our spring break the principal called me into the office and asked me if I was pregnant. I denied it. The principal told me that before I returned to school after the break, I needed to bring in a note from a doctor stating that I was not pregnant.

I had only been to the doctor once in my life and that was when I had eye surgery. I didn't know what to do. See a doctor? I had no doctor. Bush recommended the local doctor that saw black people. She went to the doctor with me, but we never discussed why I needed to see a doctor. I walked up to the counter and told the receptionist that I needed the doctor to write a letter saying that I was not pregnant so I could continue attending school. She said the doctor had to examine me. I sat silently next to Bush.

Then I was escorted to the exam room. The medical assistant asked me to take off my clothing and put on a gown. She had me lie on the table, and place my legs inside a steel chain. When the doctor tried to examine my private area, I started screaming. He asked the medical assistant to hold one of my legs, while he tried to place the speculum inside of me. I screamed louder. I told him that I did not want to be examined. He said OK, but then asked the medical assistant to have the other medical assistant come in. Next thing I knew, one medical assistant was holding one hand and the other one was holding the other hand as the doctor inserted the speculum. I heard one of the nurses say, "How did she get pregnant? She was so frightened to open her legs."

"You're definitely expecting a baby," the doctor said in a matter of fact response. I heard him, but I didn't. "Can you please give me a letter stating that I'm not pregnant?" The doctor said not to worry about it: "You just return to school, and I will call the school and speak to the principal." I walked home slowly. The pain from the examination was excruciating.

I returned to school without incident.

After I started showing, I moved in with my sister Bush because I did not want my dad to know. I was embarrassed and hurt; I knew he was disappointed in me. Bush had a room in a rooming house. It had eight to ten rooms and one shared bathroom, with no kitchen. She had a bed and a dresser.

I continued attending school and was excelling in all my classes, but I stayed on edge, in constant fear. Every time someone from the office came to one of my classes I was frightened that they were going to throw me out of school for being pregnant.

One day during class, a girl named Marion was talking with her friend. The friend said to Marion, within ear distance of me, "Marion! Is Fred still seeing Bertha?" Those words reached right into my mouth and took my breath away. I didn't flinch, and I tried to pretend I didn't hear them, but the adrenaline in my brain elevated to overdrive. Marion and her friend continued the conversation with the hopes of getting some type of response from me. This was the first I had ever heard of Fred and Bertha dating, but I knew he had dated Frances. I had heard he was also dating an older lady.

During lunch at school, I ate very little because I feared that I would vomit and everyone would know that I was having morning sickness. I continue to watch what I ate for fear of gaining too much weight and getting noticed. As I began to grow out of all my clothing, I started to raid Bush's clothing for school wear. Then she said if I wore her clothing again, she would come to school and take it off me. I kept wearing her clothes, but she never came to school.

Fred and I had sex on the floor in Bush's room. If Bush was spending the night at her boyfriend's house, Fred slept in the bed with me. If Bush came home late, she'd tell Fred that he didn't have to get up; he could continue to sleep in the bed with the two of us. Then I'd sleep at the foot of the bed. Some nights, I awakened to hear Bush say, "Fred, Betty is at the foot of the bed." For some reason, I thought sleeping at the foot and not at the head of the bed showed discretion.

We never discussed his intentions about any future with me and the baby.

By the first week of June, I was seven months pregnant. I was excited to have made it so far; graduation was only a week away. We were working on the senior play, and I had written parts for extra characters so more seniors could participate. I myself had a bit part.

One day we were doing a dress rehearsal for graduation, lining up in our gowns to enter the gym according to our height. It felt so good to finally be in that gown. But just then I was called to the principal's office.

The secretary stared me down as I tried to become invisible, practically shaking with fear. Then I was told to go in. Straight away the principal said, "Betty, you are pregnant? You are pregnant! When I called you in here before, you lied to me! You nearly caused me to lose my job!" Tears rolled down my face, but I didn't say anything.

"Yes, you did. You told the doctor that you were being kicked out of school. I didn't tell you that you couldn't attend school. Well, now you can't participate in the graduation ceremony. Here is your diploma. Go home and don't come back."

As I walked home, every tear in me was running down onto my white church blouse and even my pink skirt. To take away my school was like ripping out my heart, leaving me empty. It was the only thing that made me whole, it was my very breath. As the pain torn my heart out, I barely made it to my sister's, where I lay crying on the empty bed in the empty room, with no one to share my pain. Or to understand my pain! Bush wouldn't understand; she had stopped school in the sixth grade.

Days later, I was sitting in the car with Fred when I saw several of the excited graduates returning home in their caps and gowns, laughing and celebrating a milestone in their lives.

The pain ripped through my body again, while I sat unmoving, and unmoved.

Soon after that, Bush rented an apartment downstairs in the building our dad stayed in. I moved back with my dad, and Fred stopped his nightly ritual. Maybe he was busy with other women, including Bertha and Frances. Or maybe it was because I was not in the mood to let him enjoy my body anymore.

The summer of 1966 was hotter than normal. I stayed inside most of the day and sat on the porch only in the evenings, when the sun had gone down and no one could see my protruding stomach. I rarely saw Fred. Sometimes Christina would stop by to keep me company while I sat on the porch. Shirley stayed with Dad and me because her parents had moved out of state.

I started making plans for myself as if I were not pregnant; I was going to attend business college or West Palm Beach City College. Even if I could attend West Palm Beach City College, how was I going to afford the 50 cent round trip bus fare? So I talked my dad into going to a finance company and applying for a loan so I could attend a business school out of town. Representatives of the school had come to our school and gave a talk about it.

Dad gave me his bedroom and he moved into the kitchen. I made no other preparation for the birth of my child.

That summer, while walking to Royal's Department Store, I heard a scream coming from the third floor of the building Frances lived in with her mother. "Fred is not going to marry you!" Frances was yelling at me. I yelled back, "Kiss my ass!" and I pulled up my dress and patted my ass at her. We continued to yell back in forth until I got tired and walked on home. I don't think Frances ever had any children. I had heard around town that she had gotten pregnant and her mother had given her an abortion and nearly killed her. This is the same girl who had slept outside in Fred's car when he was in Bush's room with me.

Another time I was sitting in the car while Fred went into his mother's house to get something. Out of nowhere, Frances entered the driver's side. Just then, Fred walked out and told her to get out. "You tell her to get out!" she demanded. "No! You get out so I can take Betty home," he said firmly. Then he grabbed Frances' arm and pulled her out of the car and took me home.

I awoke late on August 22, 1966, feeling different. I started my daily routine, but around midday, I stood up to go to the bathroom and a stream of water ran down my legs. I began to feel slight pain and unusual movement in my belly. I cautiously walked downstairs to my sister's place and told her that water had gushed out of me and that I was having stomach pain. Bush said, "Betty! You are in labor!?" As I held my stomach, she took me by the arm and led me to the car.

As soon as we got to the hospital, I was placed on a gurney and was being wheeled to the delivery room, but before they could get me there a head popped out. I reached down and felt it and started screaming. I heard someone say, "Hold it! Wait!" but by the time we reached the delivery room and even before the doctor came in the baby had already been born. I heard them say, "It's a girl."

I was overjoyed to drop that load.

Fred came to the hospital and brought our daughter some clothing to wear home. He named her Freddie. Freddie was such a manly name that I decided to call her Peaches.

Peaches was a lovely, sweet baby.

Several curious people came to our home to see the baby, including two of Fred's girlfriends. Hours after their visit, Fred returned and continued his routine of having sex with me. I didn't stop him. Peaches may have been less than two weeks old.

About that time, I was sitting on the steps in our building and my dad, who talked very little, said, "Betty, take your ass back into the house. Your ass has not healed yet. I heard you and Fred in there having sex last night!" He was angry.

Those words and the sexual interaction with Fred after Peaches' birth disappeared from my memory for forty-two years. I forgot that Fred and I had sex after Peaches was born. I knew I had sex with him earlier, but not after Peaches was born and before I had the twins. This forgetting would change my life.

When Peaches was less than a month old, I remember seeing Fred and one of his girlfriends, Bertha, walking down 5th Street, waltzing down the middle of the street as if they were in a parade. But they were the only ones on the street. They were acting like they were walking on the red carpet for everyone to see. Like Angelina and Brad Pitt. They were somebody. He had his arms around her. I was fuming at this, and when I had the opportunity to speak to him I told him to come and "get that bastard out of my house before I throw her downstairs!" He came and got her the next morning. I had all her clothing packed and waiting for him. He took her to his mother, Mrs. Morales, who took over the care of our daughter.

When Peaches was about three months old, I went over Fred's mother's house. When I arrived, Fred and Bertha were sitting in the living room. I spoke to his mother in the kitchen and went to her bedroom to see Peaches. Then I went into the living room and sat down with Fred and Bertha. Bertha was sitting near the front door, I was sitting on the opposite side of the room, and Fred was sitting in the middle.

I said to Fred, "I just saw your girlfriend Frances on my way here." He pointed toward Bertha and said, "This is my girlfriend."

I couldn't believe my ears. Was this nigger that brazen? I had his baby and he was disrespecting me in front of my face and in front of Bertha? Hell no. I flew out of the wooden chair onto my feet. I was going to go to the bedroom and get my baby and leave. Then Bertha leapt from her seat, screaming, and before I could blink an eye Fred had attacked me like I was a wild animal, with fear and contempt in his eyes. By this time, Fred's mother ran out of the kitchen to see what the commotion was all about and tried to wrest Fred from killing me.

Everyone started to cry. I went to the bedroom, got my daughter, and went home, crying.

After giving birth to Peaches, I started taking birth control pills. Then after the blowout I had with Fred, I stopped taking them because I was not going to be having sex with Fred or anyone. But instead I had sex with a man named Crow for a few dollars. I used the money to buy Peaches a red dress to take her first baby picture. She was three months old. An old saying goes "Don't take pictures of a baby until he or she is three months old." She was an exceptionally beautiful baby, and smart. I should have been so proud of her because she was not only beautiful, she was an angel: she slept all night; she didn't cry; she smiled.

Crow was a taxi driver. I'd known him for years, and he had been trying to be my boyfriend for years. When I was twelve, he probably was twenty. Now I went to his room. Although I brought Norform with me, I was embarrassed to use it in front of him, and he had no bathroom in his room. He had to share a bathroom with the other tenants in the building. After the sex, when I got home, I used the Norform and douche and thought no more about him.

But before I could settle into my new life as a single mother, I started having morning sickness again.

While sitting in Bush's apartment, I feel the tingle inside my body and my pregnancy becomes more real. "How can this be happening again? What am I doing? Am I stupid? I have just written my own obituary: 'Betty came to this earth and didn't do nothin—just had babies and picked beans.'"

Oh, God. What am I going to do? What will everyone think? What will Fred think of me? What will his family think of me? What will my family think of me? My life is over. I am an absolute loser ... doomed. From this point on, my every thought will be, "What am I going to do about this pregnancy?"

I have to do something.

I flip through the pages of a True Stories magazine. Peaches is moving on a blanket on the floor. I continue to read and watch Peaches. In the back section of the magazine, I see ads for big muscles and breasts. I skim the page half-heartedly. Then, there it is: "If you are pregnant with an unwanted child, help is available." I stumble to grab a pencil and paper and start writing. "I'm pregnant with an unwanted child! Can you help me?"

Weeks later, I will receive a letter from the place stating that they are located in New York City. I will have to live there to receive their services.

MY TWINS

The nurse walked in quietly. "Give me your arm," she said sharply. I nervously extended my right arm and she took my blood pressure, the machine whirring as it filled the cuff with air and then beeping as it completed its uncomfortable task. "I need you to move forward so that I can give you a shot for the pain."

"Oh, I don't want the shot!" But she leaned over me menacingly and the epidural needle came alive, spitting fire. "No! I don't want a shot!"

I had only one memory of needles, and it was awful: when I had eye surgery as a child I had screamed through the anesthetic procedure. I had not allowed anyone to give me an epidural when I had Peaches, and I was not about to let anyone give me one now.

"Well, fine then, lie in your own pain! I really couldn't care less!" The nurse turned on her heel and left my side as I cleared my nostrils with a sharp inhale. I swear I could see a glint of sadistic amusement in her eyes. She seemed to be enjoying the fact that I was in pain.

Oh, I knew pain, and in fact I prided myself on my ability to tolerate it, but this ... this pain was more than I could bear. It was strange, foreign, alive, and horrendous. Oh Lord, I felt the pain wrack my body—I could even feel it in my hair.

I lay there for what seemed like ages, wondering if this would ever be over as the pain held me hostage in the moment, without past or future. Then, in one of the respites between contractions, I found myself thinking back to the magazine ad that had gotten me from my home in Florida to this strange hospital in New York City.

"If you are pregnant with an unwanted child, help is available." Trouble is, I would have to be living in New York City to get that help. And here I was, working in the field picking beans in Belle Glade, Florida, trying to help my dad support me and my daughter, Peaches. How was I supposed to get to New York City?

It was December 1967, and I was probably nearly three months pregnant. I felt I was in a race with time to get out of that town before anyone knew of my condition. I just didn't want anyone to know how ignorant I was. I already had one child out of wedlock; another one to me was just insanity.

Then, out of the blue, my friend Shirley mentioned that in January she would be moving to New York to live with her married sister. She said I could go with her.

I was so happy to leave.

I told my family I was going to New York to try and make a better life for myself: working and attending vocational school or college. But I didn't know how to plan things or prepare myself. I had no money, no idea what to expect, and it was only days before Shirley and I were scheduled to travel to New York that I asked my mother if she would keep Peaches. She said she couldn't. Fortunately, Fred's mother, Mrs. Morales, was overjoyed to keep her son's baby.

When I left Belle Glade, I had five dollars for food for a five-day bus trip. I had packed a lunch to take with me and I bought some food on my dad's credit at the store. I shared this with Shirley. But when that was gone I went hungry. Shirley got off the bus to buy food but didn't offer me any of it. I looked at her hungrily while she was eating, but she ignored me.

When we arrived in New York, I contacted the agency listed in the magazine ad. They told me that once I was seven months pregnant I would be allowed to move into an unwed mothers' facility in Manhattan before giving birth. So for the next few months I stayed with Shirley at the home of her sister Dorothy, in Wyandanch, New York. Dorothy and her husband, Roosevelt, had a young child, a toddler. I slept on a blanket on the kitchen floor, with another blanket to cover my body. Shirley slept on the sofa. One night I took one of her pillows for my head and she asked me to give it back. I bought my own food, but I don't remember paying any rent or being told I should pay rent. I lived there until sometime in April.

As soon as we arrived in New York, Shirley and I got a job working at the factory where Dorothy worked, making aluminum and plastic toys and housewares. The work was hard. Many nights I lay awake, wondering why I was always assigned the most difficult machines to operate. I realized later that people have to be taught to work. It doesn't come natural. And I knew how to work. I had been working since my family first migrated to New York when I was nine—first babysitting, then picking beans. I worked throughout my childhood every weekend and holiday. Shirley and Dorothy never had to work in the fields. So it made sense that I had the harder machines.

I was always assigned a machine that formed small products, which took less than one minute to form. Size mattered; the larger items took more time and the smaller items took less time to form and package. The assembling time for the small items was short, and the pieces did not have to remain inside the machine for a long time to dry.

Once you took the product out of the machine you had to assemble it together in a box. So I was constantly busy.

In contrast, a person who was assigned a machine that took five minutes to form an item could stand and relax at their machine until they would have to take the product out and place it in a box. Shirley and Dorothy were always assigned an easy machine. It took five to ten minutes for their materials to be welded together and about the same time to dry. So they could go to the bathroom, take a short break, chat with a coworker, or just stand at their machine, free and idle.

On a regular basis I sent money from this job back to Mrs. Morales to help out with Peaches. I knew if I was to get my child back from her I had to contribute to her care. But getting Peaches back was something of an abstraction to me; I mainly thought of her as a financial responsibility. Before she was born I had never imagined myself as a mother, and when I left for New York I hadn't bonded with her—I didn't know how. I simply wasn't prepared to be a real mother.

At some point that spring, I met with the agency's social worker, named Ms. Molloy. She would be in charge of transporting me to the unwed mothers' home, placing me in a foster home after the birth, placing the child in a home until adoption, and processing the adoption. Ms. Molloy was like no one I had ever known. She looked like a young Reese Witherspoon, the same height and build. Her hair may have been a darker blonde. She was very proper and educated, warm and kind. Her eyes were light brown, and she wore a tailored business suit and wore her hair on her shoulders.

This smart, attractive white woman seemed in awe of me. She couldn't believe that I had sense to want a better life for myself. "Betty, why did you want a better life for yourself and your child? Who told you to come way up here and place your child up for adoption?" I told her about the magazine ad. I told her no one told me to go to New York. It was my decision. I knew a better life was possible and obtainable because I knew that through education you could change your life and circumstances.

Beyond Ms. Molloy I kept my pregnancy to myself. To pretend I was having monthly cycles, I'd put ketchup on my clothing because I didn't want to arouse anyone's suspicion. I ate very little because I did not want my size to get noticed, but I drank milk continuously because I wanted a healthy baby. I did not have any prenatal care or see a doctor before giving birth.

Around March, Shirley and I rented a house across the street from where her sister lived. I told Shirley and Dorothy that I was going to attend school in New York City. After several weeks, Shirley moved out. By May, I had milk dripping out of my breasts, and soon Stephanie the social worker was to come and take me to the unwed mothers' home.

On May 29, 1967, the day before my twins were born, I was at home alone, waiting for Stephanie to pick me up. She was running late. Distracted, I walked into the kitchen and over to the only thing left, the refrigerator. It needed to be moved.

I had heard that you could have an early delivery if you picked up something heavy. And I didn't want to stay in the unwed mothers' home too long. I wanted to move that thing so that I could get on with the life that was waiting for me. I didn't have time to wait—I wanted it right away. So I tried to push the refrigerator back and forth, and after exhausting myself, I tried to pick it up. But of course I couldn't. Thank God I didn't go into labor until several hours after arriving at the home. I didn't know what I was doing.

I returned to my bedroom and sat on the bed. I lay down and stared up at the ceiling. The empty walls and ceiling stared back at me, keeping me company. There was nothing else to distract me.

Ms. Molloy's knock at the door roused me out of my reverie. Suddenly jittery, I grabbed the paper bag near the front door that held my belongings and followed her out to the car. We rode in silence, but a twinge of joy radiated through me as I realized that all of this would soon be over. My baby would be born and I would have the help I needed to get back on my feet.

Ms. Molloy led me through the huge double doors of the unwed mothers' home, and a nun approached us as we walked toward the office. "May I help you?" she asked in a soft, gentle, and slightly melodic voice. Her name was Sister Mary Claire, and she was dressed in the grey and white habit of the Maryknoll sisters.

Ms. Molloy identified herself and explained that she was there to drop me off. After we filled out the necessary registration forms, Sister Mary Claire took me to my room, which I was to share with another young lady. There were two single beds, each with an individual dresser, a light peach-colored bedspread on each bed, and matching curtains. I would be sharing the bathroom across the hall with the other women there. The facility could house up to twenty-eight women, and I had just gotten the last bed.

I awoke around one am the next morning with a sharp pain in my abdomen. I didn't know what to do—I felt as if a hurricane were boiling inside of me. I reached down and felt my bottom, pulling my hand back sharply when I realized it was slick with blood. Since I had fallen asleep before my roommate entered the room that night, I ended up officially introducing myself when I limped to her bed, holding my stomach. "I'm in labor! I'm bleeding!" She looked at me as if I had grown three heads, then promptly fell back asleep. I shook her awake with the hand not covered in blood. "What do I do?"

"Go see the person on duty," she said. Her blue eyes focused on me briefly, and then she turned and buried her head back in her pillow. Blonde hair lay about her head, glistening in the moonlight streaming in from the window.

I quietly limped out into the hall, blood dripping on the floor.

"What are you doing out of bed?" the nun on duty asked, setting aside her paperwork. She got up and came over to me. "Oh my gosh, you're bleeding!" She turned to another nun and asked her to bring the mop and bucket so that no one would step in the bloody mess I was leaving behind me on the floor.

The night duty nun took me to the hospital. I stood with her at the admitting desk as blood continued to seep through my clothing. The pain was steady and consistent. After what seemed like ages, I was finally escorted to a room.

Although the clock certainly continued to move forward, I felt frozen in time. The only thing that broke the monotony was the nurse peeking her head in the door to see if I was dead or alive. There were no lights in my room, only darkness. After I lay there for what seemed like days, they finally took pity on me and decided to break my water. The pain shot through my body like lightning, and I lay with my hand across my face, preparing myself for the future. I wanted to forget the procedure, the birth, the pain, I wanted to remove myself from what was going on, but they kept pulling me back to reality by commanding me to breathe and push.

Still I managed to separate myself into two parts, the top half and the bottom half: waist line up and navel down. I was completely detached from the bottom half, already disposing of all memories associated with this birthing. I kept my arms over my face during the delivery because I didn't want to see the baby. I thought if I didn't see anything, it would be easy for me to forget it all. As long as I didn't see the baby's face, it would be easy to not feel guilty about the adoption.

Then, finally, "It's a girl." She came out screaming and hollering, and I smiled with relief as the joy of it finally being over began to seep into me. But then before I knew it, someone said, "There's another one in there!" and I was being commanded to push again.

I couldn't believe my ears. "What? You got to be lying. Twins? Not me! How in the hell did that happen? Now I got to feel double guilty." I removed my arms from across my face and raised my head forward to see what was going on. I had to see for myself.

I felt thwarted. I had been so encouraged that I was able to separate myself from what was going on. Not seeing was not believing. But after the doctor's announcement, I became one again. Seeing was believing. Seeing was being, and it stuck with me, no matter what I did to shut it out.

Then: "It's another girl." I spotted a curly haired gray baby held in one hand by a nurse as she was being cleaned and weighed. The only glimpse I had of the other gray girl was her slick hair and dangling legs. She heard her sister crying and added to the sound, their voices bouncing and reverberating off the walls. They each weighed two pounds. I put my hand across my face again and immediately fell asleep.

In the days that followed I continued to separate myself into two parts: my pain, guilt, and despair were to be left in the hospital with my twin girls; the rest of me would go out into my new life. I had decided early on that I would never look back. That I would pick myself up by the boot straps and move forward in my life. It's not that I would turn my back on the twins; my immediate desire for them was to be able to support them financially. But I never thought that children more than financial support, that they need love, compassion, understanding, guidance. I saw them as needing only what I had been given by my father.

The next day I stood outside my hospital room, looking down the hall to where the neonatal intensive care unit was located. I was frozen to the spot, consumed by fear. My heart raced back and forth, calling me to walk down that hall. Then a middle-aged nurse with brown skin and thick locks walked up to me and said, "You're the mother of those twins in the nursery." I pretended that she was not talking to me even though I was the only one in the hall.

I never did make it down that hall. Later I was given a birth certificate application to fill out, and I named the girls Sonya and Tonya Owens.

I spent several days trying to get the unwed mothers' home to send someone to pick me up, and finally one of the staff arrived to take me back to the home. Upon my arrival, I found that I had no place to sleep. A girl from Brooklyn let me stay in her room and told me that I was not being treated right.

Sure enough, it seemed I had overstayed my welcome. (I felt as though I had not really been welcome in the first place.) After less than a week, Sister Mary Claire made a phone call to Ms. Molloy and asked that she come pick me up. Ms. Molloy took me to live with a foster family back in Wyandanch.

The thing is, I had no information about the agency and very little about its process. I knew that Ms. Molloy would be picking me up from the unwed mothers' home after the delivery of the baby, which was supposed to be some time after July. (She picked me up in early June.) I may have known that I would be provided a place to live, but where and for how long I had no clue. I didn't know what was supposed to happen after I arrived at the foster home. So I had made my own plans: work, occupational school, maybe college or the military.

The foster parents decided to throw me out for leaving home on a rainy day. The mother thought that I should not be out in the rain because I had just had a baby, but being a stubborn young lady, I had gone anyway. When I returned, all of my clothing was packed in paper bags and placed outside the home, and I once again had no place to go. I cried and knocked on their door, begging them to let me stay until I realized that it was futile and gave up.

I took my paper bags and walked down the street, then wandered into a restaurant. I sat down at a booth and tried to think. I had no idea what to do. I just sat there with my head in my hands, tears seeping through my fingers.

Eventually I looked around. I noticed an elderly man at the counter, who was turned around and looking at me. He got up and came over and asked if he could buy me something. I told him no. "Is there anything I can do for you?" I told him that I didn't have a place to live. He suggested a rooming house in the neighborhood. He took me there and paid my rent. I continued to visit with him until I left for Belle Glade around Christmastime.

Until then, I worked at the plastic factory where I had worked previously. I also submitted an application to join the Air Force and enrolled in a business school in Jamaica, New York. I wanted to pursue a career field on the cutting edge of technology in the 1960s: as a key puncher. I excelled in my first course, so I was hopeful.

For the practice sessions in class, the teacher assigned two students to work together and time each other for accuracy and speed. I scored 100 percent accuracy and my speed surpassed that of my partner, whose accuracy and speed was above average. On Fridays, the entire class completed an exercise. Once you completed the exercise, you put your hand up and the teacher or her assistant would come around and check your work. I always passed.

The student seated behind me was a big man, about five-ten, two hundred pounds. The seat was a little too small for him. He was not a person you would look at twice, and if you did look, he'd look away.

Every once in a while this man would say one word: "Nigger."

Whenever I looked around, he always acted like he had not said anything. I'm sure other students had heard it, but they didn't say anything, and neither did I. The teacher was aware as well, but she didn't say anything about it.

Then, after less than a month of class, the teacher decided to take me out of the situation. She had me wait after class until everyone was gone. Then she told me that I would not pass the class. I asked her to let me see the papers. She said, "I threw them in the garbage." I was shocked and hurt.

I knew she was lying, but I didn't know why. I was not a failing student—never had been. After all, in high school, I

72

could type 45 words per minute on an old manual typewriter by touch, and I had helped my mathematics teacher teach the class. I knew that I had not failed any test and couldn't understand why the teacher had lied.

What to do now?

My priorities had shifted some since the birth of my children, but I'd always wanted more for myself. Before I had Peaches, I wanted more than the necessities of life, I wanted to get whatever I desired. That meant having a good paying job that I was proud of, traveling and seeing the world. I knew it was possible because I didn't mind working and I learned quickly. Even as a young teen, I had it in my head that because I excelled at mathematics I could eventually work at the Kennedy Space Center in Florida. And even before that my song had made it to the radio. I knew what was possible by seeing Motown stars who were living high on the hog, so I set my sights high.

After Peaches was born, my goals changed. I just wanted to take care of my children financially, like my dad took care of me. The way to do this was the same: getting educated and getting a good job.

So after the business school opportunity fizzled, I took the test to join the Air Force and passed with flying colors. I also passed the physical. The examining female doctor, seeing the stretch marks on my abdomen, asked me if I had ever had a child. I told her no. I was moving forward! I was so excited about going into the Air Force. I would be trained in electronics. Not only would I live in California, which my sister Johnnie and her husband Elijah talked about passionately, but I would see the world. The way they talked, it was as if California was paved with gold, especially San Francisco. I would create a life for myself and financially support my children.

But in the 1960s, if you were not twenty-one you had to have a notarized signature from both your parents giving you permission to join the military. I sent my parents the forms to sign, and Ma signed without any hesitation. But my father refused to sign. He said, "I don't want any blood money." He thought if I joined the military I would be sent to war, and if I got killed he didn't want the insurance policy money. We didn't have a TV or radio, but the men he worked with had access to both. So he probably heard about the war from a coworker.

I then sent the form to my sister Bush, and she and her boyfriend took the papers to the notary for signature. He ran them out of his office: "You couldn't be the parents of Betty; you're only a couple of years older than she is!"

So my first two plans—business school and the military—were destroyed, and I didn't know what to do. Then a few months later I was blamed for long-distance phone calls on the plastic factory's phone bill and I was let go.

While all this was going on, Ms. Molloy the social worker had unknowingly let me slip through her fingers. Or maybe I managed to escape from her radar. The fact was, I didn't want her to know where I was because I didn't want to sign the adoption papers. I really didn't want to relinquish my twins, and I didn't want to give them away. On the other hand, I knew they would be better off if someone else raised them, and I didn't want the responsibility of parenthood. At this point in my life I wanted my freedom. I was interested in trying to make a living for myself and figured that whatever I accomplished, my children would benefit. I thought if I could stay in the picture I could support them financially.

I'm sure Ms. Molloy had the police department involved in locating me in Wyandanch because some officers went to my sister Johnnie's apartment in Belle Glade to ask her where I was living in New York, without telling her why they were looking for me. Whatever my sister told them, Ms. Molloy eventually showed up at my room. I cried uncontrollably because she had found me and I would now have to sign the adoption papers. When I recounted how I had been thrown out of the foster home she had placed me in, she said I should have contacted her. But I didn't have any of her contact information, and I didn't know that I could still get help from her agency. She told me that the agency would not use that foster home anymore.

Ms. Molloy also said that the twins were out of the hospital and were healthy and beautiful. She wanted to bring them to see me, but I knew that if I saw them I would not be able to put them up for adoption; I could not leave them as I wouldn't have had the heart to. Stephanie and I met several times to complete all the necessary adoption paperwork, and each time she would beg and plead with me to see the twins. But I always said no.

At the time the adoption paperwork was completed, I had no job, no money, and no place to live. I spent a few days with Dorothy and her family. I was back in touch with the old gentleman and I told him that I wanted to visit my family in Florida. He loaned me the money and gave me a set of Samsonite luggage for my trip.

Dorothy's husband took me to the greyhound bus station and I left New York with the same amount of money I had arrived with: less than five dollars. When I arrived back in Belle Glade, I stayed with Bush. Even though I was back in familiar territory I felt physically lost, and I was filled with an overwhelming sense of helplessness.

LOOKING FOR
MR. GOODBAR

For the next thirty years I tried to defy the odds by becoming financially secure and helping my siblings obtain the skills necessary to become self-sufficient. I reunited with Peaches, my brother moved in with me, two of my sisters and three children moved in with me. Then I married and had two boys. Each situation brought along its own challenges, and day-to-day survival became the norm for many years.

After giving birth to the twins, I went back home. I had been in Belle Glade for less than two weeks when one day, while walking to Johnnie's apartment, I saw Robert, cruising around town in a brand-new car. Robert is the brother of Roosevelt, Dot's husband, and I had met him in New York. He invited me out to a club that night in West Palm Beach. There I had my first drink of alcohol. I was nineteen years old. While riding back to Belle Glade, I decorated his car with the food I'd eaten. Robert pulled over to the side of the road and escorted me out of the car as I continued to vomit. He cleaned me off with some rags that he had in his trunk and we continued on to Belle Glade.

The next day, he stopped by Bush's house to see me. "Betty, how would you like to move with me to San Francisco, California?"

"How are we going to get there?"

He explained that his job as a United Airlines mechanic was transferring him from New York to San Francisco. Overjoyed, I couldn't believe my good fortune. But I was cautious because we first had to return to New York by car and would then fly to San Francisco once he got his paperwork from his employer. I knew he was married, but he told me he and his wife were separated.

When Robert and I arrived in New York, we stayed with Dot and Roosevelt for a few days. We then flew to San Francisco, first class. This was my first flight, and it was surreal. I was beyond overjoyed; imagine catching a genie in a bottle. More like euphoria. When we arrived, Robert and I stayed in a hotel for a few days. Afterwards, we moved in with Mr. Handy and Mrs. Louise O'Neal, his uncle and aunt. We stayed in the basement. Robert started to work and Mrs. Louise's daughter took me to Kelly Services and I got a job at California Blue Shield.

After living with them for about two months, I came home from work one day only to have Mrs. Louise tell me that Robert had moved out and reconciled with his wife. He had sent for his wife and children, and they were living in Oakland. I felt betrayed. I felt hurt in the pit of my chest.

Despite my despair, Mrs. Louise told me I had to move. Fortunately, she suggested that I rent a room in the flat where her daughter Mary lived, in San Francisco. I moved into the flat a week later.

The flat was on Haight Street, and this was the heyday of the flower children and during the height of the Black Power movement. I didn't quite get all of that at first; I was surprised enough to find that if someone rang the doorbell you didn't have to go to the door to let them in—you could just buzz them into the flat. The flat had five bedrooms, a kitchen, a living room, and a bathtub in one room and a toilet and face bowl in another room.

By the fall, I had enrolled in San Francisco City College and I worked at night.

The women who lived there were all different, but in many ways we were all the same. If the camera could have shown our lives, we would have been a number one reality hit show. The matriarch of the flat was Ms. Jones. She was a foster parent to an out-of-control thirteen-year-old who called her mother every day on the phone, yelling, screaming, and swearing. Next was Virginia, a southern college graduate queen so stuck on herself that her eyes turned inward to look at herself. Then Mary, a rebellious delinquent dropout city girl, who put on airs to project herself as being better than any of us. Then there was a secretive, attractive young woman who was hiding out and thinking she could hide her baby from us, even though you could hear the baby cry. I heard that she was an airline stewardess and her baby's daddy was a white airline pilot. Finally there was me, a country, southern backwoodswoman, who spoke worse than a hillbilly. Baby Boo Boo had nothing on me, but I had the pride of a rooster in a hen pen. So the pecking order of the flat was Virginia, Mary, the stewardess, the foster child, and me. Yes, I was last. This was Ms. Jones' standard. Mary favored Virginia, and Virginia favored me.

Virginia once took us to Oakland to a Black Panther meeting. I saw all the original members of the group. Around this time I also met Brad, the flower child. He would come over to keep me company and we would all look at television. I think he was romantically interested in me, but I guess he expected me to make the first move. He even invited me to a luncheon. I later realized they were probably socialists.

Once I felt more or less settled in San Francisco, I went back to Belle Glade and got Peaches. She was a very mature three years old. "I'm not going to call you ma because you're not my mother," she said to me. "I'll call you Betty." Once we got back to San Francisco I found her just as straightforward with everyone else. The babysitter I got to

78

keep Peaches was short lived, leaving when Peaches told the sitter's son that he was ugly just like his mother. So Mrs. Louis O'Neal became her sitter; Peaches stayed with her from Monday through Friday and came home on weekends. Peaches hated staying with Mrs. Louise; she tolerated it only because she preferred it to staying with me.

This arrangement continued until my brother Melvin moved with me in 1971. Initially I found it hard to take care of all three of us. I hadn't lived with Melvin since we were children, and at first it was like living with a stranger. I had no idea that my brother's skill level was so low, although I should have known it was because he stopped elementary school to work in the fields and take care of his siblings and help Ma.

One day I told him to go to the unemployment office to apply for work. He cried and said, "Betty, you know I can't read." My heart fell out of my body. I felt so sad.

When my brother moved with us, Peaches was three years old and I was teaching her how to read. When I noticed that she would ask my brother a word while she was reading and he did not know it, I stopped teaching her how to read because I did not want to embarrass my brother.

But Melvin enrolled in adult school and he got a job working for the State of California as a janitor. Life was looking up for us. He had passed the GED and was attending San Francisco City College.

As soon as we became financially stable, after about two years, our sister Johnnie came to live with us from Belle Glade with her three children and our sister Ann. Johnnie called me from Mobile, Alabama, where she was living with our sister, and said that she had left her husband in Belle Glade the prior week because he had hit her in the head with an iron skillet. She said that they would all be taking the bus to California to stay with me.

I was afraid to tell Melvin because I knew he didn't want them to stay with us. It wasn't until the day they were scheduled to arrive that I told him they would be there that day. Although Melvin knew I needed his financial assistance to help our sisters, he left California and returned home to Belle Glade less than a week after Johnnie and her family arrived.

After Melvin left, Johnnie took over the care of Peaches. In exchange, I gave her my paycheck to run the household, to supplement the money she received from welfare. Initially, things ran smoothly. Johnnie enrolled in adult school and got her GED. Then she enrolled in San Francisco State University, majoring in African American Studies. Johnnie's daughter, Irenis, and Ann, our baby sister, were excelling in school. Only the boys were having difficulty adjusting to the new environment.

I wanted the best for my sister and her kids. The more I did to encourage them, the more they achieved. After a year, Johnnie had progressed enormously. Then, after she started working at the postal service seven days a week, twelve hours per day during the Christmas holidays, I found myself having to accept gifts from her.

Eventually I realized that I was so involved in their progress that I had forgotten about myself and my daughter. Peaches and I were being treated like second-class citizens in our own home. Then, to top it off, I heard that Fred had gotten married. I went into a deep depression and could not get out of the bed for several months. I quit my job and stopped attending college. I even developed bed sores. I only had about four inches of hair, and I got half of that cut off.

What got me out of that depression was sheer anger. One day, I confronted my sister Ann, who was around sixteen at the time, because I had overheard her and her boyfriend having sex in her bedroom. She confronted me with a cane knife and threatened to kill me. To cool the situation off, Peaches and I went to the movies the next day, but when we returned home, Ann and Irenis had put a double lock on the door and we couldn't get inside the house.

I told Johnnie that if I got locked out again I would put them all out of the house. Johnnie went into a fume: "You're not putting anyone out. If anything, you can get out!"

I finally had enough. Here I had sacrificed my own livelihood for Johnnie, her children, and Ann. By treating me so cruelly and ungratefully, they knocked me out of the depression. The first chance I got, I moved out and left them there. I knew they would have to move because the rent was too expensive for Johnnie to pay alone. Then I got back into full gear; I returned to college and earned a bachelor's degree in behavioral science.

I was introduced to Tucker in 1974 by my sister Ann. Tucker had a job painting the house next door to Johnnie's apartment.

"Hi. What's your name?" he said to Ann. She told him and he said, "Do you have any sisters?"

"Yes, I've two sisters."

"Can you introduce me to one of them?" he said patiently, as he continued to chip away the old green paint on the Victorian house.

"How old are you?" she asked curiously. He paused, and said: "I'm twenty-eight." As she walked off, Ann said, "I'll

81

introduce you to Betty." He jumped off the ladder. "Wait! What's her phone number?" Ann told me she introduced him to me because he was closer to my age than Johnnie's. Johnnie was thirty-two and I was twenty-eight.

When I first met Tucker, no sparks flew, but he had a lot in his favor, things that I liked. He reminded me of my dad: quiet and peaceful until he had something to drink, then showing the hidden anger built inside of him. Also my sister Johnnie liked him. Another thing he had in his favor was that he told me that he had helped raise Bronda, his mother's brother's daughter, and she was a brain surgeon. But ultimately it was this: because of my own insecurities, I needed someone that no one else wanted. My primary agenda was to treat him so well that he would always want to be with me because he could never find anyone who was willing to allow him to have his own way all the time. I would essentially pay him to love me.

On our first date, we went bowling, and afterward he followed me home and stayed with me for about six weeks before returning to his own attic studio. Peaches had spent the summer in Florida, and when she returned she had a dad.

Tucker cooked, cleaned, and took Peaches to church. But I did not encourage him to get close to my daughter. Actually I think I resented it. He tried to develop his parenting skills with Peaches, but I never encouraged him.

After we had dated for a while, I told Tucker that he was going to marry me. He said OK, but he was not going to work his whole life. "I will work for about five years." I told him he didn't have to work. I was working at a day care, and I thought that I could earn enough to take care of the three of us.

So in 1976, after two years of courtship, we got married. Tucker wanted to marry me on his dad's birthday, May 13. But when we arrived at city hall it was too late to get married, so we rode all over town, trying to find someone to marry us. Finally, we went to Glide Memorial Church and Cecil Williams married us in his office. My sister and Tucker's friend, Blue, were witnesses.

After maybe less than a month of marriage, Tucker physically abused me for the first time. I'd cooked some hot dogs and did not offer him any. He knocked the plate out of my hand and said, "Don't you ever fix food and don't offer me any." I also learned that another way he used to control me was to imply that I was ugly and he was the only one who wanted me. Which is ironic because that's exactly what I had told myself about him in the first place.

We had not discussed having kids during our many talks about marriage. I wanted to be married because I had a child, and I was embarrassed to have a child without being married. I wanted people to see me as a married woman with a child because during that time, it was more than embarrassing to have a child and not be married, it was downright disgusting. You were considered less than a person. You had displayed your lack of sense before everyone.

After about three months of marriage, Tucker asked me what was taking me so long to get pregnant. Peaches was twelve years old, and although I'd continued to have unprotected sex, I had not gotten pregnant. Actually, I thought I could not have any more children, and I was happy about that. But I knew that to keep Tucker, I had to have children for him. After we got married, he said: "I want to have two sons, like my dad." So I went to the doctor and consulted with him about my chances of becoming pregnant.

And I finally did become pregnant. During my pregnancy, Tucker told everyone he knew that when I had the baby he would quit work and stay home and take care of the baby.

On March 26, 1978, I had a premature baby boy, named George Tucker Jr., who weighed three pounds, nine ounces. George stayed in the intensive care ward at the hospital until the baby weighed five pounds and was discharged to come home. By that time, I had already returned to my day care teaching job. I was happy Tucker took over George's care because he was so small. I was afraid that if anything happened to him under my care, Tucker would not forgive me.

After keeping George Jr. for about three months, Tucker went back to work and hired his own babysitter to care for our son. I did not know who the babysitter was or where the babysitter lived. Aside from that babysitter, Tucker was George Jr.'s main caretaker. He took George wherever he went. He dictated to me who, what, when, and where about any decision that had to be made about George Jr.

George Jr. and I visited my family in Florida when George Jr. was a little over a year old. When we returned to California, the baby had pneumonia and I was afraid he would die. I was afraid that Tucker would kill me if anything happened to him. Fortunately, he recovered from the illness.

I was the only one working steadily, and supporting Peaches, Tucker, and George Jr., and it took a financial toll on our lives. We became homeless often, and the children and I moved into shelters. Tucker always managed to stay with a friend, or if he was working, he lived in a hotel.

Tucker continued with his obsessive compulsive behavior regarding George Jr., and did not let him out of his sight until

I had our second son, Greg, which was six years later, on October 28, 1983.

George Jr., Greg, and I eventually moved to Richmond, California, with my sister, Johnnie. Peaches stayed in Oakland. Tucker did not move with us, but after a couple of weeks, he moved into the basement without Johnnie's permission. We knew he was staying in the basement when we heard him coughing some nights.

George Jr. was in kindergarten. Every day after school, Tucker would take George to the basement and drill him on the ABCs and numbers until Tucker was hoarse. It was a labor of love. After Tucker taught George his ABCs and numbers, when George was probably six years old, the labor of love of teaching George how to read began. Tucker never complained or wavered and never made any comments about how difficult the task was. As a parent and as the children's primary caretaker, he performed his duties diligently, with precision. And every day was boot camp for the boys, especially George.

We stayed with Johnnie for about eight months. Then we moved to our own cozy, small, secluded, two-story house. There Tucker was not only our overseer, he was the plantation owner, guarding us with relentless energy like we were his estate. I worked and the boys went to school. That's it.

George had an especially difficult time growing up because Tucker used him to his advantage. Or else you could say that he was trying to teach George responsibility. Either way, every day after school, George had to come straight home. When he arrived home, the morning breakfast dishes were waiting for him to wash. Although Tucker had been home and available all day, George had to go to the store to purchase one or two items that Tucker needed to complete the dinner. The rest of the afternoon varied: mowing the lawn, picking up paper around the yard, and so on. As George got older, Tucker took him along on his odd jobs, like painting rooms, gardening, and working at the dock cleaning out boats. I doubt Tucker ever paid George any money for his labor. However, George did become an industrious teenager. He refereed girls and boys basketball teams for several years.

From the time they were preteens until they were eighteen, Tucker took the boys to church every Sunday. Although I preferred attending a holy church and the church they attended was a Baptist church, I always felt bad that he never invited me to go with them. I did not know that George or Greg were scheduled to be baptized until they returned home from church and told me. I realized later that he wanted everyone to think that he was the one taking care of everything financially. In other words, he made out that he was a single father taking care of his sons.

Our parenting skills were completely at odds. Or maybe I should say that I didn't have any parenting skills, and I was not interested in learning, either. I was the provider, and Tucker was the parent. The arrangement was perfect for me because I knew that raising kids is an arduous job, and I should have been supportive of Tucker's parenting skills.

In 1984, I quit my current job as a clerk typist at the Presidio of San Francisco and took a long-term substitute teaching job at juvenile hall in San Francisco. Then the following year, I got another job working for the U.S. Postal Service at night.

At the postal service, I shifted into doing the heavy work, and the result was having a svelte body. I bragged to myself and anyone who would listen that I was "getting paid to look this good." And in other ways too, life was good from 1984 until 1997. I enjoyed both of my jobs, and Tucker was extremely happy to run the house alone and have both of the boys to himself. Happy days were here! I bought a home and enrolled my boys in private school. On weekends, we shopped at Safeway and Tucker and the boys put whatever they wanted in the basket. When we were not at Safeway, Greg had me at Hilltop Mall, buying him the latest toy. Tucker had a brand new truck and I had a brand new car.

We lived in Richmond, and both of my jobs were in San Francisco. So Monday through Friday, I left home around 6 am and didn't return until 1:00 am or sometimes later. So for years, Tucker had the boys and the house all to himself. The neighbors thought I was visiting them, that the house and the boys were Tucker's.

The downside was that Tucker was more controlling than ever. The children and I were not allowed to have any friends. Whenever I tried to befriend someone or vice-versa, Tucker always found something wrong with them. For instance the neighbor who lived behind us had been injured in a skiing accident, and had to use a cane to walk. She wanted me to go with her sometimes for her daily therapy exercise at the swimming pool. She even offered to teach me how to swim, and she was a writer. Tucker said, "She just wants to look at your butt." When I befriended another woman, he said, "She's a lesbian."

As for the boys, he allowed them to have one or two friends, but only as long as Tucker liked them, which was rare. Once George had a job mowing the neighbor's yard. When Tucker saw the neighbor in the yard talking to George, he told the neighbor not to talk to his son because his son had a dad and he did not need him talking to his son. The boys never had any sleepovers or spent the night out anywhere.

Several times we had the opportunity to use some of the money I was earning to upgrade our life, but Tucker didn't want any part of it. Once we had an opportunity to purchase a home in a nice neighborhood. He said no. Another time a real estate agent who owned a six-unit complex of two-bedroom apartments wanted to sell it to us and finance it himself. He said we could live in one apartment, and it would pay for itself and we would still have cash flow. But Tucker wanted no part of that, either. He knew he would be under observation, and he wanted to raise hell whenever he liked without having prying eyes upon him.

Tucker loved his job as a house husband. He still worked odd jobs, off and on gardening, hauling, and painting, but I never saw any of his money. I paid for everything. The arrangement worked out fine with me because I didn't want any part of being a parent or running a home.

But when I got injured and I was home all day in pain, Tucker and I both wreaked havoc on each other.

In 1996, as a result of my heavy labor at the postal service, I started having severe back pain and excruciating pain in both wrists. I continued in my heavy manual labor/clerk position for over a year with severe pain in both wrists before leaving work one night with a rotator cuff tear. I thought it was associated with my left wrist and stayed home, taking over-the-counter pain medication and using my sick leave. In the past the pain had usually gone away with rest over the weekends. But this time the pain didn't go away, and so after five days I finally went to the doctor, who diagnosed me with overuse of the wrists. Then on April 12, 1997, I injured my left shoulder.

Later, I was offered a job that supposedly wouldn't require using any body parts, including hands. I said to myself, "USPS will try and sell the Hudson Bridge, but not this to me." No hands? I thought they thought that I was crazy and would return to work. Whatever the job, I didn't trust myself to return because I would have done the job even if it had killed me. And I sure didn't trust the postal service.

Due to an incorrect diagnosis and delayed help from the Department of Labor, I did not receive the proper treatment and care for my shoulder injury for over six years. During the time when I could not work, Tucker was at his peak of verbal abuse. And he certainly didn't pitch in to help with the expenses. Just as before, he used the money he earned for his own addictions.

I called the police on Tucker approximately twenty times within a six-year period for threatening to beat me and for running me out of the house. Twice he enrolled himself into an alcohol treatment program, and he received temporary relief. But it never stuck. Alcohol made him angry and out of control, but when the officers showed up at our home—talk about someone who could sober up fast! He always told the officers that I had a mental problem. He was only arrested one time out of all the times I called the police on him.

I felt the only way I could survive was to get away from him. I met a woman named Darlene at a "starting your own business" workshop, and she assisted me through the hard times. She went with me to see the workers compensation doctors that the Department of Labor sent me to. And sometimes I spent the night at Darlene's house to get away from Tucker.

The other shattering loss I experienced during this time was the loss of my sister, Johnnie. She had been someone who could talk to both Tucker and me. I could tell her anything. Then, suddenly, the stability, hope, and compassion I shared with Johnnie were shattered when she passed away on July 13, 1997, from an untreated ulcer. The ulcer burst and she hemorrhaged to death. It was an unspeakable loss.

I had always been so close to Johnnie. She didn't want or ask anything of me, so it was like having an extra body, a double person to help you survive. I needed that extra body to maintain my life. The night before she died I had awakened out of a dead sleep and smelled blood. When I went to her house to check on her the next morning, she was already dead.

After Johnnie's death, I was suicidal. I missed her so much. One night while I was lying semi-asleep in bed, she came into my room wearing a robe with a hood, like Jesus Christ. She said, "Betty, what do you want now? I taught you everything I knew. I'm busy. You're going to be all right."

But I wasn't.

In August, Peaches bought my ticket and outfits to travel to Florida to be with my family. It was comforting being around my mother and siblings. Mother was distraught over Johnnie's death. I could see the pain in her eyes; it was the first compassion I had ever seen her show toward any of her girls except Cookie. We could not even mention Johnnie's name around her. She sat around all day, not eating. As much as Ma loved money, she did not want to cash the fifty-dollar money order she had received in the mail from Johnnie after her death.

I had looked forward to building a relationship with my mother and siblings after Johnnie's death, but before I could even contemplate an approach, Ma had a severe, catastrophic stroke that completely paralyzed her body and destroyed her brain. Being the strong woman she was, however, she continued to live, frozen in time, for another five years. I didn't know if she could comprehend what I said to her, but one day I said, "Mother, I forgive you for what you did to me. I was only a child and I had no business in interfering with you being with Mr. Clim." It gave me some comfort.

Losing my sister, Johnnie, my lifeline; suffocating from excruciating pain and workers compensation's refusal to pay me; living with an abusive husband; and then virtually losing my mother to a stroke was all too much to bear. I spent approximately three weeks in a mental health facility.

I could not have made it through those turbulent years without Darlene. I will always be in debt to her. I stayed over at her house when Tucker ran me out of the house at all hours of the night. Even during workers' compensation appointments for second opinions with monster doctors who were verbally abusing me for telling them about the pain I had in my left wrist, arm, elbow, and shoulder, Darlene was always there in the room, offering support.

In 1999, I escaped to Florida. I stayed with my son George, and I shared the caretaking duties with my sister Catherine by staying at the hospital with Ma. Catherine did the day duty, and I did the night duty. Catherine went to the nursing home every day, not only to see Ma but to make certain the nurses were doing their job—taking care of Ma, giving her intravenous feedings, washing her up, changing her sheets, giving her scheduled medicine, etc.

Darlene eventually told me that I should come back to California to follow up with my workers' compensation case. Also I had started having pain in my left knee. I returned to California and had arthroscopic surgery to my left knee in July 1999.

By 2001 I had started taking classes at Contra Costa College: basic Internet, web page design, and weight lifting.

In 2003, Tucker started openly carrying on an affair, going so far as staying with her for a week, sometimes two weeks before returning home. At that point I was through with him. My love was gone. When he'd come home after being gone for a week, he'd still fuss at me if I acted angry. But I just didn't care.

And it seemed that Tucker didn't care, either. In 2002, he had been diagnosed with diabetes. Not eating the proper nutrients and not taking his medication on schedule took a toll on his health. And leaving home and being gone for one or two weeks at a time without his medication added to his progressively deteriorating health, including kidney and digestive heart disease.

I had been living off and on in Alabama, but in 2007 I came back home. Although Tucker's health had worsened, it didn't stop his habits or his rage. I had to call 911 over twelve times from May 2007 until June 2008 because he had started having seizures and passing out because of low blood sugar or low/high blood pressure. During one of those calls, as the paramedic treated him and carried him out, Tucker was cursing me out. The paramedic reminded him that I had saved his life by calling them. He just scowled.

During his last hospital stay, the doctor warned him about his heart condition and suggested that he should be admitted into a hospital inpatient program for drug/alcohol treatment. Tucker refused. The day of his release, he walked out before he had received his release papers and medication. I took his medication home to him.

Two days later, in a rage, he had a massive heart attack. He died on Friday, June 13, 2008.

I'd always thought that if you give a person what they want, they will give you what you want. I gave Tucker two boys, the freedom to work whenever he wanted, the freedom to come and go as he wished. It never bothered me when Tucker stayed out one night and came home the next night. My thinking was if he found someone to treat him better than me, go for it. Plus I figured he would never really find anyone. I knew he knew he had it made. All I wanted from him was to always be with me and to never turn his back on me for another woman. But then, when he realized that he would not have a long life, he put our marriage on the line.

Since Tucker left us, the boys and I have mapped out our own lives without him. All three of us are now only beginning to live our own life.

I think about him often. Since his death, I feel free. I felt responsible for him as if he was my responsibility, like he was my child.

Peaches made the burial arrangements for Tucker. She selected a plot that has room for me to be buried on top of him. It's only five minutes away from her home, so she will be able to visit us often. And I'm sure my boys will be happy if I am buried with their dad when I die.

As for what I want, well, I wouldn't mind being buried with Tucker. I'd like to bring peace to my boys' hearts, knowing that I'm with their dad. But what I really want is that my children celebrate my demise. I want them to cry all the way to the bank. I want to leave them enough money to take care of them.

A Partial Listing

November 6, 1947, to 1956
609 Railroad Avenue, Troy, Alabama
Mother, Dad, and seven children
1956
Utica, New York
Mother, Dad, and seven children in a one-room cabin

1957
Belle Glade, Florida
Mother, Dad, and six children in one and a half rooms

1958
Utica, New York
Mother and six children in a one-room cabin

1959
Belle Glade, Florida
Mother, Dad, and six children

1959
Quincy, Florida
Mother and five children in a three-room cabin

1960
Belle Glade, Florida
Mother and six children in one and a half rooms

1960
Quincy, Florida
Mother, six children in a three-room log cabin
Belle Glade, Florida

1960
Dad, Mrs. Easter, and me in one room

1961–1962
Belle Glade, Florida
Dad, Mrs. Easter, Ann, and me in two rooms

1962–1966
Belle Glade, Florida
Dad, Mrs. Easter and me in two rooms

1967
Wyandanch, New York
*Dorothy, Roosevelt, toddler, Shirley, and me in a one-
bedroom house*

1967
Wyandanch, New York
Shirley and me in a two-bedroom apartment

May 1967
New York, New York
*Me, unwed mothers' home, one room shared with one
other person*

June 1967
Wyandanch, New York
*Two foster parents and me, plus an adult daughter in
the basement in a four-bedroom house*

July 1967
Wyandanch, New York Me, a room alone

August 1967
Wyandanch, New York
Me and a couple in a two-bedroom house

September–December 1967
Wyandanch, New York
Me, in a rooming house

December 1967
Belle Glade, Florida
Me and Bush in a one-bedroom apartment

January 1967
Wyandanch, New York
Dorothy, Roosevelt, toddler, Shirley, Robert and me in a
one-bedroom house

January 1968
San Francisco, California
Robert, me, Mrs. Louise, her husband Mr. Handy, their
two foster children, and the children she babysits in a
two-bedroom house with a basement

March 1968
San Francisco, California
Me and six others in a five-bedroom flat on Haight
Street

February 1969
San Francisco, California
Me and Peaches in a one-bedroom apartment

January 1970
San Francisco, California
Me, Peaches, and Melvin in a one-bedroom apartment

September 1972
San Francisco, California
Johnnie, Ann, Matthew, Elijah Jr, Irenis, Peaches,
Melvin, and me in a one-bedroom apartment

January 1973
San Francisco, California
Johnnie, Ann, Irenis, Peaches, Elijah, Matthew, and me
in a three-bedroom flat

December 1973–1975
San Francisco, California
Me and Peaches in a one-bedroom apartment

June 1975–December 1977
San Francisco, California
Peaches, Tucker, and me in a one-bedroom apartment

January 1978
San Francisco, California
Peaches, Tucker, George Jr., and me in a two-bedroom
flat

November 1978
San Francisco, California
Peaches, George Jr., and me in a homeless shelter

February 1979
San Francisco, California
Tucker, Peaches, George Jr., and me in a flat on Pine
Street

November 1979
San Francisco, California
Peaches, George Jr., and me in a homeless shelter

December 1979
San Francisco, California
Tucker, George Jr., Peaches, and me in a one-bedroom
apartment on McAllister

June 1980–1983
San Francisco, California
Tucker, George Jr., and me in a one-bedroom apartment

June 1983
San Francisco, California
Peaches, George Jr., and me in a homeless room in a
hotel

July 1983
San Francisco, California
Peaches, George Jr., and me in a homeless shelter

October 1983
Oakland, California
George Jr., Greg, Peaches, and me in a one-bedroom
apartment

August 1984
Richmond, California
Johnnie, Elijah Jr., Peaches, Tucker, George Jr., Greg,
and me in Johnnie's two-bedroom house

December 1984
Richmond, California
Tucker, George Jr., Greg, and me in a small two-
bedroom cottage

April 1986
Richmond, California
Tucker, George Jr., Greg and me in a two-bedroom house

Searching for My Twins

Release the shame and pain. Share it and you will begin to heal. You don't have another day to allow it to keep you captive.

Soon after Johnnie's death, I began to contemplate searching for my twins. Now that she was gone, I had to admit that she wasn't the reason I had wanted to keep the twins a secret. It was me, all alone. I wanted my family to think positively about me. I was ashamed of myself. My conscience would not turn me loose. So in October 1999, after returning from Belle Glade, I told Peaches my secret. There was no turning back. I felt free.

After I told my daughter that I'd had twins and given them up for adoption, she said, "Ma, I knew something had happened to you that you didn't want anyone to know. I thought you had killed someone because it was always like you were in so much pain." She went on to say she knew I would not have left her in Florida with her dad and grandmother for the first three years of her life if something serious had not happened to me.

A close friend of mine, whom I had known for over twenty-five years, said I always acted like I had something to hide.

I was totally unaware that this was how I was being perceived.

To this day, Johnnie's daughter can't believe that I kept the secret about my twins from her mother, who was as close to me as I was to myself. I thought I held the secret from

Johnnie because she would ridicule me. Now I realize that what I feared was not the ridicule, but what the telling would mean for the shame and pain I had carried for so long. I wanted it to be my secret. I was the one who felt the shame and pain. It was mine to own. Once you tell someone, it is not a secret anymore and it becomes a part of someone else's life. I didn't want that to happen. I wanted to punish myself because it was my fault. But I was beginning to see that I couldn't punish myself forever.

> *Guilt is a hostage taker*
> *bent on total destruction.*
> *It will cause mayhem in your life*
> *take you into a whirlwind of endless*
> *terror*
> *annihilate your every desire*
> *redirect your destination*
> *plow your heart like a runaway mule*
> *leach from you every positive thought*
> *deliberately sway your sense of desire.*
> *Ultimately it steals your soul;*
> *on your deathbed, still in ruin,*
> *it crumbles to dust.*

My spirit was ticking like a time clock. Suddenly the thing I desired most before departing this earth was to find my twins. I would always imagine them being tall, dark, and smart. I'd imagine them being married with families, working in law enforcement. Lawyers or lawyers' wives, judges or judges' wives.

I wanted to know how they were doing; I wanted to tell them I loved them; I wanted to hold them in my arms. I wanted us to cry together, to let go of the pain, the despair, and any other feeling we were having.

But I had no parenting skills, and I was not interested in learning them.

Take my daughter, Peaches. Whenever Tucker complained about me, Johnnie had always told him, "You have to be patient with Betty because she raised herself." I could say the same thing about Peaches. She learned a lot about me, from all the mistakes I made raising her.

She took what she learned from me and is an awesome parent of three independent, self-motivating, intelligent children: Antoine has a degree in behavioral psychology and is currently working on his master's in counseling. He works full time at a psychiatric hospital as a peer counselor. The average person with Rana's struggles would not have been an asset to society, but she graduated from high school, and has been working at Walgreen's as a cashier since then. She has attended three colleges and has excelled at each class she has taken. She is currently enrolled full time in a community college, pursuing a nursing degree with the intention of becoming a nurse practitioner. Twenty-year-old Leah, baby of the family, is a senior at Alabama State University. I'm always telling people, "My grandbaby is receiving two degrees: one in political science and one in the development of black pride." She is getting that second degree by observing the struggle of black families every day, especially when she leaves the school campus.

Somehow my son Greg got something from me, too. Confidence.Hard work. I drilled him every chance I got, to let him know he could be anything he wanted to be. He just had to pursue it with all he had.

When he was growing up, for instance, he knew he was going to be a basketball star. He imagined the type of home he would have: a room to hold all of his trophies, a room for his dad, and so on. He knew at an early age that he had the agility. He taught himself to ride a bicycle—no training wheels for him! He put on a pair of roller blades and soon was skating with the precision of a classical ice skate dancer. By the time he was in the sixth grade, Greg was at the top of his game in basketball and baseball.

But Greg knew you have to be realistic, too. In the seventh grade, when he returned to school after summer vacation, he noticed that several of his fellow athletes had grown three to four inches. At that point, I think he started realizing that his goal would have to be adjusted.

Yes, I had managed to pass on some of what I knew about perseverance, hard work, determination. And I was finally ready to throw off my fear and face this goal, finding my twins, with that same attitude.

When the Internet superhighway became available, I felt free, hopeful that I would find my twins. I thought if they didn't find me, I would find them. I started off by investigating how the process might work. I registered on a twins and triplets website and posted several messages. Meanwhile, I continued to surf and post messages with any other sites that emphasized adoption or searching for lost loved ones. After waiting for nearly a year with no response, I wrote the New York Department of Health and submitted my paperwork to join the New York Adoption Registry; if my twins were looking for me, the department would notify me.

But then I received a response from the Department of Health, stating that they had no record of me ever having twins in the State of New York. I read the letter several times, thinking "This cannot be true!" Could the years I spent trying to forget I had twins and placed them up for adoption have just been a figment of my imagination, a fantasy? I began to question my sanity.

But no, I had definitely given birth to twins in a New York City hospital a day before or day after Memorial Day in May of 1967. Why then were these officials saying this? Had my kids been snatched from the face of the earth?

The thing that was difficult about this was that it forced me to truly admit, on a deeper level, that I had given my girls away. To reassure myself that what I knew was true, I had to evoke from my memory every detail of the pregnancy and adoption, details I had thrown out as time had passed. I had to accept it in order to come face to face with reality.

On January 18, 2001, at 7:04 pm I received a response from my posting on the twins and triplets website. The email was from someone I will call "Jenny."

I know 2 twins (Afro-American) who have the same first names [and] are adopted. If these are your girls, they may live in [the] Pittsfield, MA area. Sonya has a daughter and travels around and Tonya was in the armed forces. Alston might be the name. ...

The two girls that I am talking about should be 30ish (?). They are not identical twins. One, Tonya, is heavy set, muscular and very "stable," went into the military. She is quiet, pensive and intelligent. Sonya is gorgeous. She is model material, medium skinned (Tonya is a bit darker). She has done a variety of things (stripper), and leads a fast life. She has a beautiful daughter which I was called upon to care for on occasion as she has some other issues that make her incapable to care for her child at times. If these are your biological twins, I can give you more specific info.

I know the mother who adopted them also adopted 3 or 4 other children ... not from the same family. I also know the adoption was done through the state of New York. I also know the kids were told their mother was alive but incapable to care for them ... and no one knew where she was. The children were told they were removed from their mother's care. Lastly, the adoption seemed to be affiliated with a religious organization. Please let me know what you want to do with this. I am indirectly involved with this family and if it would help ... I might be able to find out more for you.

- Jenny

I was so excited that I responded immediately:

Hello Jenny,

Thank you very much for the information regarding Sonya and Tonya Alston. I would like to know more about them. I will post Internet messages in the Pittsfield, MA area. Please email me any information about them.

May God Bless you

Thank you

Jenny soon replied:

Hello Betty,

Sonya (trying to create a mental picture) is model beautiful. She is very thin, 5'7" light skinned. She has dark long black hair and wears it very straight. She has awesome eyes with lashes that went to Egypt. She has delicate features. ... She is built perfect.

Tonya is heavier but not fat by any means. She is shades darker than Sonya and a different shade (does that make sense?). ... She had very thick coarse curly hair and always wore it short to medium. She was muscular but very pretty and a strong and stable looking young lady. She is very bright and more a "watcher than participator." I would be willing to bet she was the steady, stable reticent twin" <smile>... the stable force of the two ...

I would guess Tonya is 5'8", 160ish, where Sonya is 102 pounds. They are NOT identical. ... Do you know if your twins were?

I can tell you my brother's name is Paul Biagini and he lives in Cheshire, MA (a small town, Mindy is probably one of 2 black people who reside there). If you wanted to get hold of Mindy, she might be a bit compassionate and willing to help as she KNOWS what it is like to search (I helped her search for a bit). Try that. I honestly do not know Paul's number. In the interim, I will delve into my deepest mind to remember what more I might have and help in all and any ways. Let's keep working at this. This needs to happen one way or the other, BUT please don't be sad or angry if these aren't the girls. Mindy is 25ish (my bro is 46), she has one younger brother, Antoine, one older (I remembered he was 2 years older than the twins--they should be about 32 or so).

-Jenny

It turns out that Jenny knew the twins through her brother, Paul. While living with Jenny during a recuperation from surgery, Paul met a client of Jenny's named Mindy, who was one of the other children adopted by the twins' adoptive mother, Jeanette. Paul and Mindy became close and had a baby together, and they both moved to Massachusetts.

After getting further details, I finally attempted to contact the mother, and then Tonya. I wrote to Jenny about that first contact:

I spoke to the adoptive mother, Jeanette, last week, and I told her I was the biological mother of Tonya and Sonya. She mentioned all the money she has spent sending Tonya to private school and college, over $60,000. I guess she wants to be reimbursed. Jeanette said the girls appeared to be mixed with Black and Mexican or Puerto Rican and have long shoulder-length curly hair. Jeanette said she adopted the girls from Massachusetts when they were 5 or 6 years old, and that they had been in eleven foster homes before she adopted them. She said she never saw their birth certificate and did not know where they were born. She stated that she had heard maybe they were born in Arkansas. Furthermore, she said several women over the years have said that those girls were theirs. I still think that they are my girls.

I spoke to Tonya on Sunday. She was polite but very emotional about me calling Jeanette and contacting them thirty some years later. But she emailed me a picture of herself.

I asked both Tonya and Jeanette to give me Sonya's number and/or to give her my number. They each said they would have to talk to Sonya before they would give me her number.

Now, I realize that Jeanette is a liar and can't be trusted. However, I'm somewhat baffled about their color. I had pictured Tonya's complexion to be more like mine, but Tonya describes herself as being bone red (light skinned). I really can't tell from her picture her complexion. If I can recall, their dad and I had close to the same complexion, colored, chocolate. [As you can see, I still thought that Crow was the twins' father.] Like you said several emails back, about the gene pool. What do you think would be the next productive move?

Jenny, I could never thank you enough. God bless you and your family.

At first Tonya seemed excited that I called, and we talked a few times after that first phone call. But our conversations quickly deteriorated. Her every comment was, "What do you need me for? Why are you contacting me after all these years?" She felt that there was a scam: "What do you need us for—to get some money? Are we entitled to something that you want to use us to get it?" It was as if she thought I wanted to use her for something, to get something for myself.

In less than ten days after that first call, Tonya stopped all contact with me and changed her phone number.

During the 2002 holidays, I wrote a letter to my family and acquaintances:

12/26/02

Dear Family,

HAPPY NEW YEAR!

Through shame and pain, I'll share with you a secret I've held for the past thirty-five years. When I went to New York in January of 1967, I was pregnant with twin girls. They were delivered prematurely in May 1967, and immediately placed up for adoption.

I was told through a social worker that a financially secure and stable family on Long Island in New York City would adopt the twins.

Peaches and I found the twins last year. They were placed in several foster homes before finally being adopted when they were around six or seven. A lady who earned a living taking care of foster children adopted them along with three other children. When Jeanette adopted the twins they were tiny with multiple health problems. She changed their birth date by making them five years younger in order to ensure continued financial support from the state of New York. Then she moved to Massachusetts along with her male housemate, where the girls along with the other children were raised. The twins' names are Sonya and Tonya Alston.

Sonya is a single mother with two young children who now lives in Lauderhill, Florida. Life for Sonya was hard; she was sexually abused by her adopted mother's brother for several years when she was young. The adopted mother's male mate broke Sonya's arm when she was a child. School and learning were difficult for Sonya; she dropped out of high school. She said, "My dream is to meet my mother."

On the other hand, Tonya is extremely smart — a professional student. She's currently in the army in Fort Hood, Texas, studying to become a doctor. She does not want to have anything to do with me. She's tremendously hurt.

Early in January 2002, when Sonya finally did call me from Florida, she was in Fort Lauderdale, homeless. I was living with Tucker in Richmond, California; the boys were on their own by that time. I was fighting for workers' compensation for injuries sustained in my job at the postal service, and I didn't have the money to help Sonya with shelter. So I told her that if she could get to Belle Glade, about an hour and a half drive from Fort Lauderdale, she could live with my sister Bush.

When Sonya arrived at Bush's house, she brought along her baby's daddy, Ernesto; Cassandra, their three-year-old; Bianca, who was about seven; and two baby pit bulls. She was pregnant with a third child. They stayed with my sister for less than a month.

Bush told me she did not believe Sonya was my daughter. She said the only thing Sonya and I had in common was cursing. Bush said Sonya called her all type of black names.

During that time, Sonya received a back pay check from child support for her oldest child for six thousand dollars. She and Ernesto took part of the money and purchased a van and headed to my home in Richmond, along with the children and the pit bulls.

When I answered the phone, I was surprised to find it was Sonya. "Betty, our van has broken down. Can you come and get us?"

"Where are you?"

"We are in Ventura County."

"Ventura County is an eight-hour drive from here. ... Maybe you guys can rent a truck from U-Haul and drive here."

But Sonya had no money. So I called the U-Haul office myself and made arrangements for Sonya to rent a truck so she could drive to Richmond. I had mixed feelings: I was nervous and scared, each feeling overpowering the other back and forth.

They arrived in Richmond on February 13, 2002. They could not find my house, so my son George went to meet them and escorted them back to us. As they parked on the side of the house, I looked out the window. I saw Sonya get out on the passenger side. Although it was late at night, with little visibility, I could see the lightness of her skin and the long silky black hair hanging on her waist as she reached in the cab of the truck to get Cassie out of the front seat. Ernesto walked around the truck to help them. Bianca followed them into the house.

Sonya and I hugged and the rest of my family greeted them warmly. When Sonya went into the kitchen to get Cassie some milk, I followed her. Sonya was leaning over the sink, washing out Cassie's bottle. I took my hand and moved her hair out of her face so that I could see her eyes.

When our eyes met, I had no emotion. My eyes became like the lens of a camera, trying to focus, trying to find something that would identify this child as mine. I looked at Sonya until I felt a spark of light that communicated compassion and warmth. At that moment, I felt that I was looking into my daughter's eyes, those eyes that I had yearned to see. The light that I saw was my reassurance: she was enough for the moment.

Then my eyes pulled back for a full view. Long black silky hair reaching below her shoulder blades, very fine facial features: small pointed nose, lips so tiny, high cheek bones, and large glacial eyes with eyelashes extending to the South Pole. Seeing her made me question my own sanity. Everyone's yelling, "Who's the mother?" while I'm questioning, "Who is the daddy?" Thirty-five years is a long time. How could I justify Sonya's appearance? She didn't look anything like me or my family.

But Peaches called me daily from work and said that Sonia looked just like me. That music brought happiness to my heart. But I still wondered: should I go with how I feel or what I think? If Sonya and Tonya were not my twins that meant there was hope that my real twins were adopted by the nice family on Long Island I had been told about all those years ago. There was hope that they had enjoyed a wonderful life. I said to myself, "You wish, Betty. But will you be that lucky?"

112

We gave Sonya our bedroom and we slept on the couch in the living room. Three days later, I set them up in a sixty-dollar-per-day extended stay in San Ramon. Then, after exhausting all my money, Sonya and her family moved in with Peaches. In these early months with them, I found out that Ernesto had often been in jail, usually for driving without a license, driving under the influence, or possession of a controlled substance.

After staying with Peaches for about two months, Sonya moved in with my son George and his girlfriend Frances in Stockton. While living with them, she talked their landlord into renting her an apartment for a thousand dollars a month, with no job or income. I paid the rent for two months, after which time Sonya and her family moved back to Peaches' house. With the help of a friend from the postal service, we threw Sonya a baby shower for her three girls.

This is how things were with Sonya.

On March 14, 2003, Sonya and I each took a DNA test. I demonstrated to Sonya how it should be done, and Sonya gently swabbed her mouth. I didn't think she had supplied enough saliva to be tested, but I didn't say anything. I just mailed the test off and waited for the results. They came after nearly thirty days; the letter stated: "It is 99.9% certain that you are NOT the biological mother of Sonya Alston."

I let the information resonate in my brain for a couple of days before I told anyone. When I finally told Peaches, she said, "Mama, can we keep her?" My son Greg, on the other hand, questioned me on my decision to spend money on someone without a DNA test. He said, "Ma! You get the DNA test first, and then you spend money. It's like putting the cart before the horse." He had no idea how desperate I was to reunite with my children; a dog could have shown up and said, "I'm your child" and I would have accepted her.

Soon after that Ernesto cornered me and said, "Is Sonya your daughter? What was the DNA results?" I hesitated for a second, trying to compose my thoughts and emotions. Then I told him that Sonya was not my daughter.

I cried uncontrollably all the way home after hearing myself admit the truth, although I made every excuse possible trying to make Sonia my daughter.

Sonya and Ernesto returned to Florida with their children several months after the birth of their third child, Victoria. By this time, Peaches was happy to take them to the airport. She dropped them off and didn't look back. I guess she was relieved to get herself and her mother off the merry-go-round Sonya had put us on even before she set foot in California. Now Sonya, Ernesto, Bianca, Cassandra, and Victoria were all safely in Florida.

After several months of living there with no work, Sonya and her family found themselves homeless again. Ernesto's mother put them up in her home for several weeks. Sonya had a fourth girl. For a time, they lived in Miami in an apartment for twelve hundred dollars a month, but still neither one of them had a job.

By that time, which was late in 2004, I had moved back to Troy, Alabama, and was living with Ms. Johnnie Mae Warren and Dr. Eddie B. Warren. Sonya contacted me in Alabama and said that they had moved out of the apartment in Miami and were back living with Ernesto's mother. But Ernesto's mother had told Sonya that although Ernesto and the kids could stay with her, Sonya could not. She was spending different nights with tenants at an extended stay hotel. She asked me if she could come to Alabama to stay with me.

114

I may have said, "If you can get here you can stay with me." But I wasn't concerned about her coming to Alabama because I knew she did not have any money to come and I was not going to send her any. What I didn't expect was that Ernesto's mother would rent a van and drive Sonya and the four girls to Alabama in a severe storm.

Now Ms. Johnnie Mae had a three-bedroom, one bath property that we called "the blue house." The exterior paint was cracked and faded, the interior walls were unpainted, and the carpets were shabby, stained, and odorous. When Sonya and her family arrived, Ms. Johnnie Mae told Sonya that she could stay in the blue house.

But Sonya refused to live in the blue house, which she said was not up to her standard of living. So Ms. Johnnie Mae allowed them to live in the guest house in the back of her home. I paid Ms. Johnnie Mae three hundred dollars a month rent for their stay.

After two months, Ms. Johnnie Mae told me Sonya had to move into the blue house. Sonya got angry; "If Ms. Johnnie Mae put me out of the house, I will call the police and report her for child abuse for putting me and my three children out on the streets!"

So Ms. Johnnie Mae hatched up a scheme to get Sonya out. She said that she was going to be out of town and everyone had to leave, including me, even though I was like her daughter and was living in the main house with her. I went along with it and spent the night in a hotel, and sure enough, Sonya moved into the blue house.

I did everything to make Sonya comfortable there. And she knew just how to intimidate me to make that happen. One day, while the handyman was fixing the toilet, she cursed me out and threatened to beat me up, yelling that she was not accustomed to living in these conditions. She ranted and raved for about thirty minutes, putting on a show for the handyman and for my cousin, who was also there. I agreed to replace the toilet as well as the bathtub, stove, and refrigerator.

I also ended up buying a washer and dryer and lots of furniture, including brand new bedroom and kitchen sets. I had the walls painted and replaced the wall-to-wall carpet. I continued to pay Ms. Johnnie Mae the monthly rent. I also paid Sonya's utilities and phone bill, and even gave her spending money.

Why, you are probably asking, did I put up with all this?

Although by this time I knew Sonya was not my biological daughter, I needed her. I needed her to fill the empty hole in my heart. At this time I was not as hopeful that I would find my real twins. And after being around Tucker all those years, I had become accustomed to accepting all responsibility, being an enabler for situations I had nothing to do with or no control over. For example, Tucker knew how to make me feel guilty and sad about the way his parents treated him while growing up. He would remind me that his mother made him do all the housework chores while his brother Sonny didn't have to do anything; that his cousin, the babysitter, physically abused him daily; that his mother rarely came to the hospital while he was hospitalized for months at a time for a severe kidney disease. So I put up with his abuse.

In a parallel way, Sonya verbally attacked me and made me feel that the living situation was my fault because I was the one who had told her she could come to Alabama. And since her condition was my fault, I had to take care of her. As with Tucker and other people in my life, I allowed her to take advantage of my stupidity, or my kind heart.

116

Ms. Johnnie Mae knew I was paying for everything, and she didn't think I should. So she took me to the housing authority to get Sonya into the projects and out of the blue house. This was a little less than a year after Sonya arrived in Alabama. We followed through with the housing department on a weekly basis, and Ms. Johnnie Mae patiently and kindly coached me into not taking responsibility for Sonya and her children.

When Sonya received the notice that she had been assigned housing in the projects, she hit the roof. But with Ms. Johnnie Mae's help and encouragement, I stood up for myself, telling Sonya that she had to move. Around August 2006, I left Troy to visit California. When I returned in September, Sonya had moved everything out except the kitchen sink. When Ernesto was released from his current sentence, he moved into the projects with Sonya. Two months later, Sonya was pregnant with their fifth daughter.

Eventually Sonya got in a fight with one of the project tenants and the lady hit her with a forty-ounce beer bottle. As a consequence, the housing authority gave Sonia a Section 8 certificate so she could move out of the projects. She and her family moved to a rural area several miles from Troy. They would stop by Ms. Johnnie Mae's house sometimes to get money.

For the next three years, Sonya worked odd jobs: gas station-cashier, clerk at various fast food places. Ernesto stayed home and kept the kids. Whenever he got angry with Sonya, he would show up at her job and cause her to get fired. The last I heard, Ernesto had returned to Florida and Sonya and her five children still live in Alabama.

I could not look at you, but I could still
see your face.
I could not hear you, but the scream was
loud and clear.
I could not touch you, but I could feel
your warm embrace.
I could not smell you, but the scent was
mesmerizing.
I could not taste you, but I savored the
sensation.
Yearning for you!

After the DNA test told us that Sonya was not my biological daughter, I felt less hopeful about finding the twins I had given birth to. Yet every time I got on the Internet, regardless of what I had planned to do, I would end up on a site that had everything to do with searching for an adoptee or loved one. I posted on every registry that had anything to with adoption, especially in New York.

The State of New York still insisted that there was no record of me giving birth there. So I turned elsewhere. Among the places that turned out to be scams was a service called Givenright. Someone there named Jennifer told me she had information on my twins and needed payment. I sent it by Western Union (it was under five hundred dollars), and the next day, Jennifer contacted me with new information.

She said one of the twins was a chemical engineer and had her own business in Staten Island. She was married, but with no kids. She taught dance and was close to her adoptive parents and grandmother, who all lived on her block. Jennifer said the other twin was in Iraq. Apparently the twins had been separated when they were babies because the mother who initially adopted them couldn't take care of both of them.

I really wanted to believe this story. When I asked for contact information for the twin who lived in Staten Island, Jennifer gave me the run-around of my life. "The twin does not want her information disclosed," "The twin fears her mother will have a heart attack if she knows the birth mother is going to be in touch with her," and so forth. I eventually realized it was a dead end, especially when she stopped taking my calls.

Then in early 2004 I paid Snoopers, a website that claimed to find missing persons, to search for my twins. They found two girls listed on the New York birth index under the name Owens, born in Manhattan on May 30, 1967. They also had the birth certificate numbers: 16694 and 16695.

Once I had the numbers in hand, I considered traveling to New York to visit the Main Library, where the birth index census records were available to the public. I knew that if I found their numbers on the index I could also find their adoptive names. But I didn't get the opportunity to make this trip.

Then came 2007, a year with one small but significant break in my search for the twins.

It started out the same old way—fruitless. On March 27, 2007, a letter from the State of New York Department of Health arrived in response to my latest query, dated March 8, 2007. It read: "The adoption Registry has been unable to verify that your twins were born in New York State. The New York City Office of Vital Records was unable to find their birth certificates and the Catholic Home Bureau has no record of handling the adoptions. Regrettably, we have been unable to obtain any documentation of your children's births or adoptions. Without this documentation, the Adoption Registry is unable to assist you."

Undeterred, on April 3 I wrote them back, providing them with the birth certificate numbers I had from Snoopers. On May 22 they responded, stating that with the additional information I had provided "we will resubmit your requests to the New York Vital Records Office and Department of Social Services."

On May 25, I received a letter from New York Office of Children & Family Services. They informed me that if both the adopted child and the birth parent were registered with the Adoption Information Registry, the registry could help facilitate a reunion.

On June 5, I received a letter from the City of New York, Administration for Children's Services, Division of Legal Services: "We are in receipt of your request for your records. Please be advised that we have made a diligent search of the Administration for Children's Services (ACS) files but no record for you or your twin daughters, Sonya and Tonya, has been found. Accordingly, we are unable to comply with your request."

On August 15, I wrote the Adoption Information Registry, New York State Department of Health, to update them with the information I had received from Jennifer at Givenright.

Finally, on December 31, 2007, I received a letter from State of New York Department of Health, Vital Records Section. They verified that that my children were born and adopted in New York State. My name had been placed on the Adoption Information Registry to await my children's voluntary registration. I was assigned a registry identification number.

During the Christmas holidays in 2008, I received an email from a personal search company called Kinsolving, stating that they were offering half price for their service and if they could not locate the person there would be no charge. I said to myself, "What do I have to lose?" I signed up and sent the only reliable information I had, which was the twins' birth certificate numbers.

Within two weeks, I got an email stating that they had found my twins. The letter stated, not surprisingly, that to get the information, I had to make the payment.

I believed, yet I didn't believe. How could it have been so simple for this place to find my twins when I had spent years trying? I told them I could make only a partial payment at that time. They said, "OK, we will take the partial payment, but we will not give you the information until we receive the entire payment." I agreed and sent the whole amount in two payments. Two days after I sent the second payment, I received the adoptive parent's name, Sonya's and Tonya's telephone numbers and mailing addresses, and information about family members who were also adopted by the adoptive parent.

Armed with another set of phone numbers, I found myself afraid to call. I thought about all that had happened after the last time I made this kind of call.

After a couple of days spent trying to build up my confidence, I picked up the phone and called Tonya. A drowsy female voice said, "Hello?"

"My name is Betty Owens, and I'm your birth mother." She hung up the phone in a heartbeat, without saying another word.

I had two telephone numbers for Sonya, and a few days later I called both. I left a message on her phone and said that I'd been told that I was her birth mother and that I would like to talk to her. Then on February 10, 2009, Sonya returned my call.

My first impression of her voice was that she was really a New Yorker. She listened to what I had to say, but with very little apparent interest. She told me that she would send me a picture of her on my cell phone. When I received the picture, it was like looking in the mirror. The resemblance was so absolute that it scared me numb.

I sent her pictures of myself, and she told me her friends said that there was no need for us to get a DNA test because we looked just alike.

After that, we talked several times a day. Mostly we talked about me and my family. Occasionally, I told her about my siblings, but she was not interested in hearing about them (and still isn't). I told her that I was sorry, but I had made the best choice available to me.

I make arrangements to travel to New York to meet her. I arrived on April 13, 2009. I took a red-eye flight, but I couldn't sleep. It was a nonstop flight to New York, and the plane seemed to arrive so fast I didn't have a chance to compose myself. I had to put myself in a dream state to confront my fears, hopes, and dreams.

Sonya's friend Marie met me inside the airport while Sonya remained with the car. When we got there, Marie put my luggage in the trunk. I opened the car door and got in. Then I reached over and gave Sonya a hug as she sat in the driver's seat. She gave me a dozen red roses. I think neither of us could feel happiness or pain at this point. We were on auto-pilot.

I cried on our way back to her apartment, not for Sonya or for me, but for the sake of Marie, her friend. She was sitting in the back seat, keenly observing our every movement and every word of our conversation. I couldn't see her face but I could feel and hear her thoughts: "Here is this woman who has not seen her daughter in forty years and yet she is not showing any emotion." So I cried for her sake, to demonstrate my love for Sonya.

The feeling of being watched, of being on stage, didn't stop there. Sonya drove us directly to a diner, where she said more friends were waiting for us. When we arrived, Sonya's friend Rosa was standing outside, smoking a cigarette. We greeted her, and then Sonya, Rosa, and I posed while Marie took pictures. Inside the diner, four more of Sonya's friends were waiting for us. They motioned for us to join them in a corner booth.

I felt like her friends were observing me through a surveillance camera, like Sonya needed their personal approval to have a relationship with me. I was trying to impress both them and my daughter, to convince them that I'm not a hard, selfish person. I started feeling self-conscious about what I was wearing, about every word I said.

Sonya and I sat next to each other in the diner. We held hands and hung onto each other, and everyone smiled and expressed joy at our reunion. Rose announced to the diner customers that Sonya and I were meeting for the first time in forty years; several of the people came over to greet us. Rosa mentioned that we should contact the media to come out and do a write up about our reunion.

During the rest of the three-hour meeting, I didn't volunteer any information; I just answered whatever question they asked. Why did I give the twins up for adoption? How did I find Sonya? Did I have any other children? How long was I going to stay in New York? They seemed fascinated, eager to be witnesses to this unusual event. They were intrigued by the way I talked, astonished at how much alike Sonya and I looked.

Over the course of the morning several of Sonya's other friends stopped by to meet me. I felt so obligated and I wanted so much for them to like me that I offered to pay for everyone's breakfast. They objected, and one of them collected enough money from each of them to pay for the meal.

This scrutiny continued throughout my visit. One evening we went to visit a friend of Sonya's named Mary Ann. She earned a living taking care of five mentally disabled females, all white. Mary Ann projected herself as Sonya's keeper: "I'm not going to allow you to take advantage of Sonia." She acted like I was some type of scammer, trying to beat Sonya out of something by trying to take advantage of her.

I started to cry. "I would never take advantage of anyone, much less my own child." The good thing from all this is that on that day, I finally got a sense that my behavior proved to Sonya that I was sincere and that the only thing I wanted from her was to give her whatever emotional healing I could so she could live her life with less guilt and shame.

The visit was not easy. Each time Sonya and I had a disagreement about something it scared me to death—I didn't want to lose my daughter again! And we did have disagreements. Once Sonya said to me, "I'm used to giving advice and having people do what I say. But with you, you love to listen to what other people have to say, but in the end you do exactly what you want to do." I could say the same thing about her.

But we slowly let down our guards. We went shopping, for instance, and she picked out several outfits for me to purchase for myself. I also bought her a sweater and a blouse.

One thing I can say about my daughter Sonya is that she has played the hand she was dealt. Her adoptive mother told the girls that their mother didn't want them and she had just walked out and left them in the hospital. But I grew to see Sonya as a strong, self-sufficient woman. It appeared that she is living the kind of life she wants to, except for not completing her nursing degree. Some people let their circumstances dictate their life, but Sonya lives the life of style she desires.

But Sonya does camouflage her personality. She can act like she is illiterate or mentally retarded. I think it is just a front; she does it as a defense mechanism, in order to get a head start on other people. Her close friends think that front is who she is, but I know that Sonya does not do anything that she does not want to do. It may take her longer than the average person to get out of a difficult situation, but she knows when to hold and when to fold.

So she is unlike the rest of my family. Most of us play the game of life, especially with love, until it is drained and there is nothing left but pity, or insanity—a pain so horrible to live with that our personality splits. We let another person take over the pain and we take on the personality.

So I think Sonia got her attitude partly from how she was raised. Her adoptive mother adopted and raised five foster children; the twins were the youngest. From pictures I've seen of their mother, she appeared to have been mixed. The three oldest children also appear to have been mixed race.

The mother told the twins that they were Haitian. She probably told them that because black people were not giving up their kids for adoption in 1967—especially twins, which later I heard is supposed to mean good luck. In black families there was always an aunt, grandmother, or neighbor to take care of a child. Outside adoption was not an option.

The mother raised the last two, my twins, as a single mother because her husband had died. Since it was just the three of them, Sonya was treated as the male of the home. She had to do all the hard physical work, like removing the snow from the yard during the winter and walking from the store with heavy shopping bags. She said, "I never complained because I lived to please my mother."

Her sister Tonya, on the other hand, lived to please herself. Initially, it appeared that Sonya grew up as Tonya's big sister, that she always felt she had to protect Tonya because she was tiny. Sonya grew up thinking she would always have to look after her little sister, be her protector. But she told me that Tonya could be cruel, because of the difference in their appearance. Sonya was always heavy set and Tonya was always slim and trim. She said that Tonya did not even want her to walk home with her after school.

They lived in an all-white neighborhood and attended an all-white public school. It appears that Tonya felt right at home in that environment. She was on the debating team, and she took part in other school activities. But Sonya struggled with learning. She showed me one report card that was filled with Cs and Ds. She probably has dyslexia and she may have been in special education classes.

After Sonya graduated from high school, she trained to be a certified nursing assistant. Afterwards, she immediately began to work. The mother kept her uniform starched and ironed, and she took Sonya back and forth to work every day. Initially, she waited at the job site for several hours and would go and do some shopping and return to pick Sonya from work. During this time Tonya was attending a university in New York City, working on a degree in economics. Their mother grew old, but she still took care of them like they were teenagers.

The girls stayed with their mother until she had a stroke and had to be cared for in a nursing home. In other words, Sonya and Tonya did not move out of the home until they were in their thirties.

After the mother died, the house had to be sold to pay the unpaid bills. So the girls were finally forced to live on their own. Sonya told me that she gave her share of the inheritance to Tonya because she had been accepted at a college in Pittsburg, Pennsylvania. This seems true, because Tonya's goals were to please herself, while Sonya lived to please the mother, even after she died.

I think hearing about Sonya's adoptive mother—how she mothered the girls and how Sonya lived to please her—I think that intimidated me to some extent. I'm not a mother; I'm a parent. I will give you money and listen to your desires and offer opinions on your direction according to your desire, but as far as being a mother goes, that is something I've never desired to be. I should be ashamed of myself for saying that, being the parent of five children.

I always wanted more than that. After my experience with the nuns in Utica, New York, I wanted to become a nun so I could help people. Then I wanted to become a mathematician and work at Kennedy Space Center. Then I wanted to become a writer. I never wanted to be a mother.

One of the positive thoughts that kept me sane was that the twins had each other during the dark days. But that was a mixed blessing, and now they are more isolated from each other.

Tonya has lived in Pittsburgh alone for the past eight to ten years. She has not invited any of her family to visit her, and I have a feeling if they showed up she would not let them into her apartment. To be honest, I think Tonya has inherited more of the family DNA. In other words, functional mental illness.

Recently, Tonya has been showing up at the train station unannounced for Sonya to pick her up, and she will stay with Sonya and wreak havoc on Sonya's life. Tonya becomes like a rebellious child around Sonya. She refuses to put on a seat belt while Sonia drives. She gets paranoid; she moved out of her apartment because she thought one of the female neighbors was watching her. No one is allowed to ask her anything about her life: jobs, friends, etc. The other family members don't want to make her angry, so they always comply.

On occasion Tonya travels from Pittsburg to New York City, which is an eight-hour ride on the train, to update her wardrobe with coupons at some of the high-end stores. I can just imagine her traveling on the train looking luscious, but daring anyone to speak to her or show any interest in her. In other words, she loves attention and she knows how to get it, but she won't let anyone get close.

Sonya has never had sex, has no children, and has never been in a long-term relationship with anyone. Sonya said Tonya is also a virgin, never had any kids, and has never been in a long-term relationship with anyone except for an email friend; she communicated with him over several years, but she never talked to him or saw him.

Tonya likes to participate in marathons, and she likes to help serve food at shelters during the major holidays, like Thanksgiving and Christmas.

Sonya's passion is her work, counseling, but she also loves hanging out with her friends over dinner.

Sonya told me that Tonya doesn't want her to say anything about me to her. Sonya always says, "Tonya will talk to you when she is ready. She is not ready yet."

LIVING MY OWN LIFE

When we can no longer change a situation, we are challenged to change ourselves.

—Viktor Frankl

As I write this, Peaches lives in San Pablo, California, where she is a medical records manager. George Tucker Jr. lives in West Palm Beach, Florida, and is a journeyman piledriver. Greg lives in Las Vegas, trying to map out a life to live like the rich and famous. Sonya Jones lives in Happaguage, New York, where she is an LPN, and Tonya lives in Pittsburg, Pennsylvania. She works various jobs, such as customer service, accounting, or bookkeeping.

As for me, I've been living with Eddie B. and Ms. Johnnie Mae intermittently for almost ten years. It started back in 2004, when Eddie B. was taking me to the airport after a visit. He said, "Betty, if you come back and be my mother's companion, I'll take care you for the rest of your life; I will provide food, shelter, and a car." Since then, I've returned to California at least five times with the intention of never returning. I lived in California for nearly two years during this time, from May of 2007 through April 2009. But for the past three years I've been back with the Warrens in Alabama. Recently, Eddie B. started taking to referring to me as his daughter's stepmother, and now he refers to me as her mother. Even Elaine has started referring to me as Eddie B.'s future wife. He has expressed his desire to marry me to another family member. But I'm always silent during these conversations. He has not mentioned his intentions or his plans to me, other than by saying he will honor his promise.

What I do know is that this time with the Warrens has elevated my self-esteem to an all-time high. Living with them has afforded me an opportunity to grow emotionally, and of course writing this memoir has been better than therapy. I feel like I am just beginning to live.

I realize how blessed I am; I'm responsible only for myself. The few people I know who are in their fifties or sixties are already prepared, or are preparing themselves, to take care of their parents, or their grandchildren. But me, I'm sixty-five, and I'm ready to live my best life. I've decided that I'm going to be happy, with Eddie B. or without him. I'm happy with who I've become.

Who have I become? That's like asking, "Who am I?"

When 50 Cent was talking to Oprah about who he is, he said, "With my grandmother and myself, I am Curtis, but my persona with the world is 50 Cent. Sometimes I have problems cutting 50 Cent off." Similarly, life has instilled a distinct difference in what I am, depending. I can be Betty Owens and I can be Betty Tucker.

Betty Owens is self-assured, sharp tongued, and extremely critical of others—the sky is the limit on that one. I can do all things through this Betty. She will make a way out of no way. Like the time when she was driven to New York City to take a Greyhound bus to Belle Glade, Florida, and didn't have enough money to buy the bus ticket but still managed to pay the fair and make it to Belle Glade. Betty Owens is the product of her upbringing: tough, hard-working, and no nonsense.

And then you have Betty Tucker. Life has taught her some important lessons since she was a young woman: You are who you think you are; you become what you believe; whatever you feed will grow; you've the power to become the hero in your own life. This Betty wants to fulfill God's promise.

131

Betty Owens still believes she can conquer the world; however, Betty Tucker knows that time is not on her side. Betty Owens knows the Lord can move her to the front of the line to receive her blessing. Betty Tucker is realistic; all dreams are not to be conquered because once you obtain one dream you replace it with another dream. Maybe both Betties would say, "Never try to forget your dreams. Even if you do try, they will never allow you to forget. They will hang on in more damaging ways."

It seems like the rest of my life will not start until I complete my journey with Mrs. Johnnie Mae. When she trusted me with her life by saying she wanted me to be here for her in her last days, it stole my heart.

Now don't get me wrong; it has been a challenge. When Ms. Johnnie Mae's daughter, Elaine, moved in with us in the latter part of 2006, staying with the Warrens began extremely challenging. Elaine and I started butting heads right off.

"Betty! Don't use the guest bathroom. It's for guests. Use the bathroom in your own room!"

"Elaine, if I'm near the kitchen and the bathroom is right across the hall, why do I have to go all the way to my room to use the bathroom?"

"Well, you can't be using the bathroom all over the house. I use the bathroom that is in my room and you should do the same."

Another time she said, "You should not boil the eggs with the potato to make the potato salad. That is nasty. The eggs have all types of germs on them. You should boil them in a separate container." Or "Who used the microwave and left it running after pause? You need to clear otherwise it will continue to scroll." Or "Don't put cold water in a hot iron

132

skillet because it will warp. ... Don't wash your hands in the kitchen sink. Use the sink in the utility room or your own bathroom sink. ... Don't use metal utensils in Teflon because it will remove Teflon. ... Whenever you leave your bedroom, leave the door open so the air can circulate. ... Don't have your mail sent here." Eddie B. put his foot down on that last one, saying, "Betty can have her mail sent here."

Like I said, over the past nine years, I've moved back to California at least five times with the intention of never returning to this life with the Warrens. But being away brought only temporary satisfaction. Nothing compared to the experience I feel being around Eddie B. and Ma. I feel secure, protected, and loved. I know I can make it the final chapter of my life—living and being of dedicated service to the Warrens.

So says Betty Tucker. But Betty Owens says, "What's in for me if I opt out of this situation now? No compensation, just feeling I've been used." Betty Owens doesn't trust the Warrens. She's doesn't trust people at all. When everything is said and done, Betty Owens can always hear Bush humming in her ear, "I told you so! Those people don't care anything about you; they are better than you and they will never let you into their lives. You dummy! You think Eddie B. wants you? That's where the color line comes in." And frankly, I don't know what would hurt me the most: Eddie B. not wanting me, or feeling like I was just used. He told me one day that if his Ma didn't like me I would not be here.

I know how the world thinks: "White is the perfect color." The darker you are, the farther down you are, and my dark skin puts me at the bottom of the pecking order. But I didn't grow up thinking that if a person is light skinned they are better than me. Forget that Eddie B. is a doctor. So what that I'm dark skinned. I'm just as intelligent as he is.

One day I was in front of Ma's house sweeping the entrance way near the crosswalk and a lady approached me and said, "How did you get to stay here?" My thinking was not how I got to stay here, but how fortunate they are to have me.

So, let me say it again: whatever happens, living with the Warrens in Alabama has afforded me an opportunity to love myself, to build healthy self-esteem, to forgive myself, to look forward to a productive future. In other words, living with the Warrens has given me the opportunity to reflect on my past and build a future. Through our relationship I have grown to understand and accept that you cannot control the attitudes of others; I have begun to learn how to not allow others' attitudes to affect my goals as I journey through my life.

A decent and good life needs to develop a GPS, what they used to call a "moral compass." It will help you when you stop at intersections, where you have a choice to make. At each intersection, you have several factors to reckon with in deciding which direction to take, such as your DNA, your upbringing, your peer group, your desires. You also have to look at any barriers that stand in the way in either direction. You have to listen to your conscious conversation with yourself but also to be aware of your unconscious conversation with yourself. All of these will impact the decision you make about the direction you take.

In the Wizard of Oz, Dorothy knew which direction to go, but she lacked the confidence to find her way home. Many of us are like this. So we wander in the wilderness for years, like the Israelites, trying to find our way home.

While listening to Oprah's Lifeclass with her guest Joel Osteen (my favorite spiritual healer), I tried to absorb words as a part of my journey to find a direction for myself. The theme of the show was "Whatever follows, 'I Am' will come looking for you." What is needed to allow this to happen?

I've often thought that I pursued my goals or desires with nothing available to me but faith alone. But now I realize that along with faith, I did everything in my power to seek the desired end. I knew from the time I was a young child that if you want something, you pursue it with all you have. For instance, while working at the postal service I decided I wanted to be a supervisor. I knew that at the time, an unattractive, dark-skinned African American woman in the San Francisco Postal Service had a better chance of hitting the lottery than of getting promoted to supervisor. So how did I do it? Was it faith alone?

No. I did have faith. But I also had a degree, and most of the supervisors didn't. I was willing to work my butt off. I aligned myself with a supervisor who could help me reach my goal. I got promoted, and I wasn't too shy to tell people what a great feat it was. And then, when I realized that being a supervisor would mean giving up my day-time teaching position, I relinquished my promotion to become a clerk again. People thought I had lost my mind. But I had simply replaced one dream with another.

How did a poor, poverty-stricken girl come to be where I am, to value the things I value? Perhaps I haven't always known it, but I have always operated under the principle that I'm better off than the next person. Things don't identify who I am. My heart tells my story.

I was born this way. I came into this world demanding what I wanted. Even as a young child, I knew something. My Auntie Juanita once said to me, "Betty, me and Alto always talked about what you've become. Because even as a child you walked around switching like you owned the world." I demanded that someone rock me to sleep every night from my earliest memory until I was six, seven, or eight. And I got rocked to sleep! Not only did I get rocked to sleep, but I demonstrated how I wanted to be rocked, and got it. Never mind that I had two younger siblings. When Honey Gal was busy with one of the other children, Ma had Johnnie rock me. I was a demanding child, and this gave me an advantage.

I'm also resilient. Let's face it, much of my life has been like the reality TV show "Wipeout." For every situation, I had to overcome hurdle after hurdle, to find my way in a forest without having the guidance of parents. What is so sad about not having guidance from a parent is that you pass the same lack of guidance onto your children. It is not enough to inadvertently teach them to do as you do. You've got to do more, to actively parent.

Since my siblings and I were neglected and abused as children, we tend to go overboard with our own children. It becomes double duty: you try to ensure that you give to yourself in ways your parents never did by supporting your children too much, always being there to give financial help. This prevents them from growing up and becoming self-sufficient. Yet even with all the support, they continue to make a difficult future for themselves by being single mothers and continuing to have children. They compound their futures and their children's future, just like we did.

Ma and Dad separating had a ripple effect on me and my siblings' lives—such an effect that we are still trying to make amends to ourselves through our kids. If Ma had left Dad for a single man, maybe it would not have had the traumatic outcome that it became. However, the man she dedicated the duration of her life to was just as dedicated to his other family as to her.

Ma's behavior had a profound effect on all of her children. I'm not going to blame all the mental illness in our

136

family on her, because I know we have inherited the genes from both sides of the family. But I will say that the way each of us has dealt with our significant other or spouse is a duplicate copy of Ma's interpersonal and social behavior, namely, completely losing all common sense.

In our relationships, we tend to crave love so much that we become willing to sacrifice our own life and family to please the other person, just so that they will stay with us. We even go beyond what is humanly possible. Is that what takes us to the edge between fantasy and reality? I think so.

Another significant consequence of Ma's behavior is that many of her kids had to stop elementary school in order to work in the fields year round, picking beans to take care of themselves. Only two of us had high school: me, because I left to stay with Dad, and my oldest sister, who had graduated from high school before we migrated to New York. It was only later that any of the others began to catch up, and I believe that was partly through my influence.

After the success my brother Melvin experienced living with me in California—learning how to read, finishing high school, attending college, and working for the state of California as a janitor—he was finally able to return to Florida and pursue a career, becoming a two-ton trailer truck driver. He in turn supported and encouraged his wife to return to school, and she received her high school diploma and took evening college courses. She is one of the managers of a health clinic.

When Johnnie moved to California with me, she was able to complete her high school education and went on to attend San Francisco State University. When she left she was only twelve units shy of a bachelor's degree in African American Studies. Then, with a twenty-five- year career at USPS, she started an upward mobility with her children and our other siblings. Her daughter has a master's degree and has a six-figure job.

When Ann came with Johnnie to California, she was also able to graduate from high school. She obtained an associate degree from San Francisco City College before moving back to Florida, where she worked for the state as a supervisor in the food stamp office. My brother Sammy and his wife also moved to California, where he acquired auto mechanic skills. When he returned to Florida he pursued further training and is now a bus mechanic supervisor of the school bus system in the area. His wife remained in California and pursued getting her GED and completed a certified nursing assistant program before returning to Florida.

So all in all, we were all affected by our past, but we continue to be influenced by the decisions we make every day. Our pasts didn't stop us in our tracks.

Of course the past still touches us, no matter how positive we become. Take money for instance. Even now I have to guard who I associate with because I allow people to use me. When people realize how free I am with my money, they hang on for dear life.

Maybe I just like being liked. But it's also that money doesn't mean that much to me. I've never needed money or things to make me happy. Over the years I've willingly shared money with my family, especially Bush. Ten years ago, I paid the outstanding bills for her and Ann to clear up their credit so that they would qualify to purchase a home together. I even paid the down payment and closing costs. As recently as one year ago, I paid Bush's car note and one hundred dollars a month on her car insurance. I stopped paying only after I realized that I should not be paying for her car when I didn't have a dependable car for myself. Plus an acquaintance had told me that I should be saving my money in case I have an emergency. I never thought of that before.

So it's partly just not knowing what to make of money. I use it to give it away. I read somewhere that the feeling of pleasure you get giving away five hundred dollars is equal to that of receiving five thousand dollars, and I guess I believe that. I love the feeling I have when I give, especially to my family and loved ones. This is true even if I have to sacrifice my own well-being. Now I realize that does not make any sense. Like the stewardess says at the beginning of a flight, "In case of emergency, put the mask over your own face and then assist the baby or toddler." I am still learning this.

Since Sonya and her five daughters still live here in Alabama, I would like to have a relationship with them and help them. I know that being an unskilled mother of five children is financially difficult. But I can't afford to spend money on them that I don't have. I texted her this past Christmas and wished her and her family Merry Christmas. I was glad she texted back and said simply, "The same to you," without asking for anything because I would have wanted to help her.

I don't know why I feel the way I do about money. Maybe I think I don't deserve my own money; I feel guilty for what success I have had. Or I feel sorry for my family and want to help. Or I'm just downright stupid. Or I'm just chronically responsible. Ever since I left Alabama when I was nine years old, I have felt responsible for someone or something: paying the rent, water, gas, food, telephone, babysitter. The only time I wasn't responsible was when I was living with my daddy.

Knowing that our DNA and our upbringing affect our decisions might make it easier to forgive ourselves for our mistakes. We learn as we go. Some of us have fewer tools to begin with, so we have more to learn. On the other hand, it's not good to lean on this as a crutch. We've got to own up to our actions—to claim our mistakes as well as our successes.

When I relinquished my twins, for instance, I really thought that I could go on with my life and it would have no effect on me. Boy, was I wrong about that! As much as I tried to pretend that I had never given birth to them, the more they haunted me. I carried an invisible load my whole life, and it affected my spirit in ways that are still becoming apparent to me. I have had to admit that the decision to give them up had a huge impact on everyone. And I have had to face those consequences, in all my relationships.

Even so, I must say I'd not do anything different. Once you start thinking of what you would have done differently, you hinder your progress in moving forward with the knowledge you learned over the years. No one is born with a GPS or a Master Key; you take what you are given from your relatives and your community and make up the rest as you live.

One thing I've allowed myself to imagine is what my life would have been like if I had known that the father of the child I was carrying (the twins, as it turns out) was Fred, Peaches' dad. Not knowing this had a lot to do with my not wanting to keep the child, and keeping those babies would have been a pivotal point in the direction I'd choose to proceed with my future. In other words, if I'd known that those twins were Fred's, there would have been no way I'd have relinquished them.

As I recall, what really motivated me was the thought of Fred knowing that I'd had sex with and was pregnant by someone else. It was something I refused to face. I simply refused to put myself through the shame of unwed motherhood again, to face the consequence of my actions.

The deeper truth is that by keeping that baby (the twins, as it turns out) I would have sealed my fate and future, and not in a good way. I would have become a duplicate copy of Ma and my sister Johnnie. Like Ma, I would be hopelessly in love with a man who didn't care about me at all. (When I left Florida for New York that January, Fred's other girlfriend Bertha was already pregnant and showing with his child.) I'd have been dedicating my life to service for his attention. Like my sister Johnnie, I would have worked in the fields, packing corn or celery, to take care of all the kids that I'm sure I would have had for Fred.

And the real truth is that if I'd stayed, I doubt my life or circumstance would have affected Fred in any way. Bertha or no Bertha, babies or no babies, he ended up capturing the attention of a college preacher's daughter and grabbed for the opportunity to upgrade his life by marrying her. They moved into the married student dorm until she completed her college degree. He just sailed into the sunset, waving farewell to the broken-hearted Bertha. And he would have been me left behind as well.

So I can honestly say that I'm glad I didn't know that the twins belonged to Fred.

Of course, our decisions affect our children, some more deeply than others. I did not know this when I became a parent; in fact, I knew very little about parenting. Nor did I want to. As a child growing up, I never dreamed of becoming a mother with kids, a husband, and a house with a white picket fence. My dream was to be an explorer and travel the world, to live in California, to use my gift in creative writing to earn lots and lots of money.

So when I had children, my upbringing dimmed my vision about the direction I chose to raise my children. I took my dad's approach to raising a child and ran with it. Dad saw his role as a parent as being the provider. I, too, saw that as my total responsibility: nothing less, nothing more. Shelter and things would be all they would need to become responsible human beings. I figured if I could grow up this way, they would, too. Boy, was I wrong!

I think the most important thing I've learned being a parent is that you have to decide if they will be your investment or if you will invest in yourself. Do you pay while your children are growing up, or will you pay when they become adults? What I mean by "pay" is the investment in their future: teaching them positive social skills, responsibility, even just reading something about parenting skills.

For instance, I had one major opportunity to change the direction of my children's life, but instead I invested my decision in myself and my own desires. Before giving birth to Greg and becoming homeless, I had the opportunity to move to waterside community of Benicia, California. It was a nice place, with good schools and safe neighborhoods. But I didn't take it.

Here's what happened: While living in a homeless shelter, the organization selected their most promising client to help. They choose me because I had a permanent job. They connected me with two housing options: an apartment in Benicia or an apartment in Oakland, California.

I chose the apartment in Oakland because it was more convenient: Tucker could take dependable public transportation to visit us, and I wouldn't have to find another job. (My commute to San Francisco would have taken up to three hours one way on public transportation from Benicia.) Actually the owner of the building in Benicia had told me he could get me a job working for the city. But I didn't want to change jobs.

This decision had an immediate effect on my children. Ever since I took Peaches back from Belle Glade when she was three years old, she and I had a tenuous relationship; now that gap widened. While I struggled to put food on the table, she was busy mapping out her life, and not in the direction I would have chosen for her.

In our three-story apartment building there was only one other person who worked, Kevin, a young man who lived on the second floor with his single mother and siblings. So Peaches didn't have to go far to find friends. My commute to work starting me off at 5:30 am, and I didn't return home until after 6 pm every day, giving Peaches plenty time to socialize.

One evening, a school truancy lady stopped by to find out why Peaches had not been attending school. What's worse, when she saw my baby Greg, she thought it was Peaches' son. It was news to me that Peaches had not been attending school. I assured the woman that Peaches would be returning to school.

Eventually I succeeded in helping Peaches, as well as Johnnie's son and daughter, in getting a job at the Department of the Army at the Presidio of San Francisco. But Peaches had other plans. She moved in with Kevin and his family. Months later, she was pregnant.

The Benicia community is still thriving. In that community my children would have had a better future, good schools, a positive living environment, and positive role models. Who knows how things might have gone for Peaches if we had lived there during those difficult high school years?

Being a good parent requires sacrifice. Again, you have to decide if the children will be your investment or if you will invest in yourself. What many young parents don't know is that if you don't pay while your children are growing up, then you will pay when they become adults: in watching them commit crimes, become incarcerated, get pregnant out of wedlock. You'll pay in their lack of job skills, their lack of self-esteem, and their lack of direction for their life.

Investing in your children's future does not mean buying them toys or even paying their tuition. It means looking at the bigger picture. I spent plenty of money sending my sons to a private elementary school, but in reality I should have used that money to purchase a home in a better neighborhood. I assumed that if I was able to make some sound decisions in the neighborhood that I was brought up in, they should also. That was the worst decision. Thinking like that is like leaving your children out to dry.

Fortunately for us, even with all of the demons Tucker had to deal with in his life, he still tried his best to be a responsible parent. Tucker was the teacher of wisdom; he tried to equip his sons with the tools they needed to become law-abiding, productive citizens. He joined the church and the boys got baptized; they had curfews and chores. They did their homework every night, and Tucker bonded with them during their nightly games—chess or checkers or just sitting in front of the TV looking at sports. He helped them plan: George was going to pursue a military career in the navy and Greg was going to attend college. These are just a few of the things that create a healthy upbringing.

Throughout my marriage to Tucker, I was the breadwinner. During our early years of marriage, I told him he wanted me to purchase the cake and he only wanted to contribute the icing/frosting on the cake. But working two jobs and being gone all day never bothered me because I didn't want to have anything to do with running a household or taking care of children. I guess it didn't bother me because it was not the type of life I wanted to live.

So my decision about what kind of parent I would be still affects me. I'm away from my children. I hinder their growth by continuing to support them even when they are adults. I hinder their dreams by selling them my dream: "I'm going to be a big-time published author." That is my dream; it is not theirs. Everyone has to have their own dream. A parent should be supporting the children's dreams as well as their own. But as my children wait for me to fulfill my desire and passion, they are putting their own dreams and life direction on hold, especially my son George.

Once at a parent conference George's teacher told me that during a class discussion, she had asked him what he wanted to be when he grew up. He said he wasn't sure if he was going to stay home and keep the children or pursue a job. After the teacher finished talking, she paused for me to respond, and I just looked at her and didn't comment. But I knew that George's answer came from how life was in our household; I worked and his dad was a house-husband.

But I can also see that George is gradually letting go of this idea. He is contemplating marrying Frances, whom he has had an on-again-off-again relationship with for over fifteen years. He also thinks that one day he will have full custody of his son from a previous relationship, and he knows that he will have to work to take care of him. He is gradually letting go of the idea of us being together, of me taking care of him, because he sees that I am making a life for myself.

My goal in life has always been to leave an impression on people. I try to leave them with something to think about, something that will bring about growth in their own life. Maybe that's why I am a good teacher. Plus I like working with the underdogs. I liked to sell the kids I worked with a dream, because they were not dreamers. They considered themselves losers—that's why they ended up in juvenile hall or the other projects where I taught.

My approach was to raise expectations, to work with students individually and to expect that they would exceed all the expectations that people had previously had for them, which were low. I knew I'd made an impression on the students when they asked, "Are you sure you know this is a special education class?" I always pretended that I didn't know what they were talking about; I assumed everyone knew they were smart and capable of doing much more than they had been doing.

Because if you believe in yourself, you're half way there. This is what I try to tell myself when it comes to writing.

During those lonely country days along the red dirt road on a tobacco farm in Quincy, Florida, sitting on the porch with nothing in sight and nothing on my mind to distract me, I wrote the lyrics to "That's the Sound of the Men Working on the Chain Gang." You might remember this story from chapter 3.

When I first heard my song on the radio, I immediately recognized my lyrics. At that point in my life, I knew I could write; I knew there was a better life out there waiting for me. By the time we moved back to Belle Glade, I heard another one of my songs being song by one of Motown's leading women's groups. This song had fewer of my words, but the theme of the song was exactly the same as mine. Then I started writing poems about seasonal hurricanes, and I read them to the class. I loved the praise and accolades from the teachers and students; I loved the feelings the poems bestowed upon my self-esteem. All this happened while I was still in elementary school.

At that point I saw a blink of hope that my writing talent could lead me out of poverty. But that was short lived, since I had little support in becoming a writer and little understanding of how the world works. Instead I was learning that if you are poor and powerless, people can just take whatever they want of yours and do whatever they want with it.

Only during my last year in high school did I write anything else creative. The senior class performed a play; I added a couple of extra characters to the play so that more seniors could participate. I did not attend the senior play, so I don't know if the characters I created were performed.

Then much later, when I was living in San Francisco, I wrote a poem about Martin Luther King, Jr. It was after his death. The poem was inspired by one of the Black Panthers meetings I attended in 1968. I submitted the poem to the party to have it published in their newsletter. Later, in 1973, when I was working at Bank of America, a fellow employee there told me she had read my poem. I was shocked because I had never seen the poem in print. She said it was printed in one of the Black Panthers books, one that was sold to raise funds for the school breakfast program they had started in Oakland. She asked me if I wanted her to bring the book to work so I could see it. But I knew if that book with my poem in it was brought to work and management saw it, I would have been fired on the spot because it was a radical, brutal poem, similar to the initial teaching of Malcolm X.

I was surprised at the whole thing—surprised that they liked it enough to publish it. I hadn't even kept a copy; I didn't see any value in it. But throughout the years, whenever I was in the neighborhood, I have stopped by Marcus Book Store in Oakland to see if they had a copy, without any success. I wanted to see it in print.

At about that time, when I had graduated from San Francisco City College, I was accepted into the TOPS Program at San Francisco Catholic College for Women, which later was renamed to Lone Mountain College after they started accepting male students. This was a program that helped minority students with potential to obtain upward mobility/education.

My dreams of being a writer were eaten up by the need to survive—work, school, taking care of everyone. And they were also crushed by my growing knowledge about what success as a writer would entail. One day, I was walking across the college lawn. The buildings were set on a large hill, overlooking the serenity of San Francisco. There I saw an African American student, being filmed while practicing a news report. He sounded so fluent with standard spoken English, so polished in his bearing. At that point I completely gave up my dream of becoming a writer. It seemed that to become a writer you had to major in journalism, and with the problems I was having with grammar and my southern speech, I abandoned my dream on that hill.

In my younger years, I had imagined my creative talent would be my ticket out of poverty. But then life happened, and I didn't do any creative writing for thirty-four years. From the time I wrote the poem about Martin Luther King Jr. until 2002, when I started taking writing courses, I didn't write, except what I had to for school.

Then, in 1992 or 1993, I was teaching at a pregnant minor program in San Francisco. A volunteer came once a week and taught creative writing, using art to enhance the students' self-esteem. She was a student from the University of San Francisco. (I heard later that she became a professor and taught at USF.)

During our commencement ceremony that year, I was chosen to be the guest speaker. I wrote an inspirational speech individually acknowledging each student's gifts. The creative writing teacher edited the speech. With that process, I again saw a sparkle of creativity in me.

In 2002, when I started taking computer courses at Contra Costa College, I noticed that creative writing courses were available at Vista College and Berkeley City College. I signed up for a creative writing course and was hooked.

I realized then that I had not lost my writing talent. Reading some of my creative writing in the classes I was taking and seeing how the instructor and students reacted, I surprised even myself. In one assignment we had to read "A Rose for Emily" by William Faulkner and write an essay of our thoughts about the poem. I wrote a four-page story about Tobe, Ms. Emily's servant. I was so overjoyed with my creativity that I asked one of the students to read aloud a couple of passages from my story. The students were in awe!

But I struggled with grammar, and so found it difficult to write. Not knowing things like whether the verb I had chosen was the correct tense could stop me in my tracks. Furthermore, I could only write when I was taking a writing class. When assignments were given I would write, but when the class was over I stopped writing. I suppose I liked the attention I received from my writing by the instructors and students. Plus it's just hard to keep going when there is no deadline to force your hand.

And then it's difficult to ignore the voices of those who would stop you. They mean well, but their voices stop you with "reality," with all the obstacles in the way. When I was in my late forties I told a dear friend, who was like a mother to me, that I wanted to be a writer. She responded, "You're too old to start a career in writing." I listened. For awhile.

One time I told a good friend, "Regardless of where you are in life, the Lord can put you at the head of the line." She said, "That doesn't make sense." Her words tried to stop me right there. But I can't live without that hope.

About five years ago, I told another lady that I wanted to be a writer. After listening to me for several minutes, she said, "You missed your calling."

I said to myself, "What an awful thing to say to someone. I'm still alive. As long as you believe you can do it, you can."

I do believe that. It's not magic—it takes hard work and good fortune. But I believe it.

As businessman and author Robert G. Allen says, "Don't let the opinions of the average man sway you. Dream, and he thinks you're crazy. Succeed, and he thinks you're lucky. Acquire wealth, and he thinks you're greedy. Pay no attention. He simply doesn't understand."

One thing I take away from this life is appreciation for all who have passed. I've always felt blessed and shown favor from the Lord because of all the people that I've lost; that I've always been gifted to spend precious time with them.

It started with my dad.

Once I went to visit my family in Florida. I believe it was late in the summer of 1979. I brought George, who was about fifteen months old. Dad was very proud of his grandson.

One day we went to visit Dad's friend. We had to walk up about twenty-five steps to get to his place. Dad wanted to carry George up the steps himself. I was afraid that he would fall, but I allowed him to carry George in his arms as I walked behind them, thinking, "If my Dad falls I can protect them."

For the entire two weeks I stayed in Belle Glade during that visit, I went to work with him every day, stacking sod. I had never gone to work with him or stacked sod before. We laughed and talked as we worked. He told me jokes. I had not had a conversation with him like that since Ma was pregnant with Mr. Clim's daughter and I tried to convince him that it was his child.

My dad gave me shelter from the elements in the streets. He provided me a safe house. He showed me unconditional love even though I was not his favorite child. Johnnie was his favorite.

A Tribute to Dad

You gave me hope
I received self-reliance
You gave me your heart
I learned to love
You gave me values
I learned morals
You taught me faith
I became a believer
You gave me compassion
I learned empathy
You taught me wisdom
I learned insight
You gave me life
I will forever be grateful

Then there is my sister Johnnie. She had a constant battle with demons, but sustained enough energy to show me unconditional love throughout our lives. For all her troubles, she listened to me. Our conversations were always about my problems. I talked nonstop, and she listened, attentively, to my every complaint. And man, did I complain, mostly about Tucker.

Every Sunday, Tucker cooked dinner for the family, including Johnnie. She worked on Sundays at the U.S. Postal Service, and she always stopped by to eat dinner and lay down on the couch before she went to work. Tucker always fixed her lunch to take with her to work. I think they understood each other.

A day or two before her death, I remember saying to her, "Johnnie, is there anything I can do for you?" She said, "No, I'll be okay."

Then, out of nowhere, she went on to say how she saw me. She saw me as thinking I was smarter and brighter than any of my siblings, and that I always tried to be a step ahead of them. She thought I wanted my children to excel ahead of their children. Johnnie probably also thought that I was making the incorrect choice in trying to succeed at whatever I was trying to do. She thought I lacked common sense. "If you would have just taught school instead of also working at the United States Postal Service you could have made a name for yourself teaching school."

A day before her death, I had visited her home. She looked at me as she lay in bed. She appeared to be sick and had given up on living. Once she told me that there was nothing on this earth that she was interested in doing. I said, "Johnnie is there anything I can do for you?"

I wished I could have told her how much I loved her. She was really the sunshine of my life.

That October after her death, I suffered from severe depression before becoming suicidal and being hospitalized. I thought about Johnnie a lot. One night I was lying in bed, semi-awake. Johnnie walked into the room wearing a white robe that went from her head to her feet. It was angelic. She said, "Betty what do you want? I'm busy. I've taught you everything I know. You have the tools to continue your life without me. You're going to be all right." Then she turned and walked out of the room. Sometimes still I find myself hearing her say, "Betty, you're going to be all right."

I didn't attend Johnnie's wake or the funeral. Tucker, my daughter, maybe my sons, and Johnnie's brother-in law from her first marriage also attended, and her son and his wife came from Florida. Everyone asked where was I because they knew how close Johnnie and I were. But I didn't want to see her dead. I always wanted to remember her being alive. Moreover, I didn't want any of her coworkers and friends to see me fall apart at the funeral service. I was not going to give them that privilege. My daughter took pictures of Johnnie in the casket, and it took me years to even look at those pictures.

Whenever I dream of Johnnie she is always alive.

Johnnie did not gossip or lie.

Next was Ma. I had visited her in the August right before Johnnie's death. When I came back home to California, I stayed with Peaches. One day, while sitting on the floor, I found myself crawling to a Bible resting on an end table in my room. I opened it up and prayed for God not to take my mother. For the next several weeks I went to the store nearly every day. I took a twenty-dollar bill with me and I bought gum or a piece of candy, usually spending less than five dollars. When I got home, I put the change in an envelope and sent it to Ma. I had no control over my behavior. That process became a ritual.

I didn't know my mother, but after thinking about her all I have to do is take a look at myself and I can find her.

Hazel would do whatever she wanted, even if it killed her. What other people thought about her, she really didn't care. Hazel lived her life.

Although Ma was eighty-three when she had the stroke, I'd never seen a gray string of hair in her head because she kept it colored a reddish auburn color. Even during my visit with her in 1997, after Johnnie's death when Ma was distraught, she got up every morning wearing a floral dress and smudge of reddish lipstick across her lips.

Hazel liked the outdoors, and she liked books. I was told that she named me after a character in a book she had read. And the weather conditions didn't interfere with her daily routine. While it was thundering and lightning, she'd be sitting outside, reading the daily newspaper. She came inside the house only when the wind blew the rain on her.

Hazel was quiet. You never knew how she felt about you because she showed little emotion, if any. When Dad died, I came back home crying. I hugged Ma to comfort myself and she returned the caress with no expression. What's done is done; you can't go back. She never worried about the past. She never complained about anything. Every day was a new day with its own adventures.

The only time she showed emotion was when she had to ask you to do something. Hazel wasn't a beggar; it hurt her to ask for anything. She hated to ask even little things of you, even if it wouldn't cost you anything. Like she hesitated to ask me to go to the store for her during my few visits to Belle

Glade. And the few times she asked me to go to the grocery store and buy something on Dad's credit when I was a child, it was never to get something for herself, but to get something for one of the children.

Johnnie always told me, "Betty, can't no one tell you anything." That was how Ma was. She just kept her kids moving, following Mr. Clim, all for her sake. My brother Sammy said he told Ma that he was tired of migrating to New York every year doing season work picking beans. I didn't ask him how many more times they migrated before she decided to stop.

Hazel didn't teach values, morals, or anything to help her kids along life's journey. She gave us nothing that we could reach back and use in times of indecision. You were on your own. I guess she was on her own, too. Although Ma was at least twenty-five years older than her children, she navigated her existence just like her children: with no use of past experience to lead the way. They were in it together. All she did was decide where they would go and they all pulled together to make due in the situation.

I'm also grateful to my girlhood friend, Barbara. And Shirley. They have taught me that friendship is a two-way street. You have to be going the same direction; otherwise, the other person will pull an unexpected fast one, which will leave you wounded. Barbara was a good friend. She was my best friend; although at the time I didn't know it.

On the other hand, I came to find out that Shirley was never my friend. Barbara and I were just her stepstools. I realized this after finding a shoebox of pictures in Fred's mother house. In one of them, Shirley is standing with Bertha and Fred and one of Fred's friends; they were on a weekend luxury hotel double date. She was out with Fred and Bertha while I was pregnant with Peaches! What's worse, it was

155

during the time that she was staying at my home because her parents had moved out of state!

I've forgiven Shirley and tried to develop a friendship with her over the years, but she hasn't shown any interest in rekindling our friendship. On the other hand, Barbara always came to see me on my few visits to Belle Glade after moving. During my last visit with her she said, "Betty, it's not a day that goes by that I don't think about you."

While returning home from Sunday church service in 1999, Barbara was killed when a two-ton transfer truck jackknifed into oncoming traffic and crushed her auto. I was visiting Belle Glade when it happened, and I changed my departure date so I could attend the service. I called Shirley when I heard about Barbara's death, to share our loss; she just said "okay" nonchalantly and hung up.

These girlhood friendships illustrate an important truth. Like Oprah says, "If a person shows you who they are, believe them." My friendship with Shirley taught me to be cautious with your heart because your friend may become your enemy. People are human. They are not perfect. They will lead you into temptation and turn their back on you if you bite. Never say, "Oh, that person wouldn't treat me bad." Remember, according to the Bible, man does not know his own heart. So how could you honestly say that any person will always be compassionate toward you?

Then there is Ms. Johnnie Mae. I will be forever grateful to her. She taught me that you're never too old to live.

When I started visiting Ms. Johnnie Mae, she was eighty-four years old, and I was deeply depressed. Every day, she got up and lived her day as though she had found the solution to eternal life. She groomed herself like she was participating in a beauty pageant show. She mowed her lawn. She was active in various community organizations. Every Christmas she got up on a ladder and hung her own ornaments outside her home.

She gave me the opportunity to live again by being supportive, encouraging, and loving. For example, when I was scheduled to take the teacher's test to obtain an Alabama teaching license, she got up at six o'clock that morning and cooked me a full-course breakfast. When she ate a sandwich, she split it in half and encouraged me to take the other half. For our daily outing, if I slept late, she came to my room singing, "Wake up little Susie, wake up!" I would turn over on my back, smiling and stretching like a baby. She gave me the opportunity to live again, to see value in myself, to dream again.

I also want to thank Honey Gal, who rocked me to sleep every night.

And Peaches, who showed me who you are doesn't necessarily reflect your complete embodiment but includes the fruits you harvest. She is grooming her three children to become the best that they can be. She realizes that maturity is more than an age; it's circumstance that takes responsibility to the next level of your development.

To My Fifteen-Year-Old Self: Things I Wish I'd Known:

I don't think the Lord put us here on earth to spend our entire life struggling to make ends meet. The Lord also gave us the Garden of Eden to enjoy. He gave us love for pleasure. He gave us our hands, arms, legs, and brains to share in this wonderful experience on this earth. We have to learn how to share because everyone is not created equal, and I'm not talking about race, creed, color, or religion.

I love this quote from Craig Lock: "God, the Source of Life, will never give you a desire, a vision, an individual dream without your having the ability/potential for it to come to pass." I try to believe that.

What is so interesting about living is that you only see and understand things after they have passed, and then you can't go back to correct or change. As you look at your past, the future holds the unknown, which will challenge your wisdom further.

But when you're young time stands still. That's how we are wired. Things like life and death, like danger—they don't matter to us. We think bad things happen to others but not to us. Like you can't tell a drunken man that he should not drive because he may get in an accident and kill himself and maybe others. He won't believe it. That's similar to our heart, our emotions, our passion, ourselves—especially when we are young.

When we are caught up with emotions: love, friendship, desire, wants and needs, our minds become like a feather in the wind. We will go along with it, not thinking of circumstance or consequence. We feel it must be right because it feels right. I'm not here to tell you to "say no to sex." I'm here to inspire you to desire more.

You may not believe it, but I once was in your shoes. I was ten years old, eleven years old, twelve years old, and thirty-five years old. And all along I've been in love: once when I was twelve, again when I was fifteen, again when I was eighteen, again when I was twenty-eight, and again now, and I'm sixty-five. For some of us, it never ends. We should count ourselves lucky.

When I was young I fell in love with a boy. I knew I was in love because when he looked at me I got a chill through my spine; I laughed. The feeling was something I had never experienced before. It controlled me; my common sense was gone. I could get pregnant but I didn't care; I was in love. And I didn't care how he felt about me! All I knew was that I loved him.

He liked me, but he didn't want anyone but me to know it. Was he ashamed of me? Was it my hair, my clothing, my teeth, even my feet? I tried to figure it out so I could change it. That was a learning experience.

There is no quick fix for withstanding your desires. Your mind becomes like riding in a merry-go-round; you become dizzy. But here's one thing to remember: the way you feel about him (or her) is not permanent. It will not last forever. The way you feel about him probably will not last passed your next grade. Then it will be someone else who steals your heart. Even if you marry and stay together, your love will change. Your feelings will change.

Remember that, and it will give you strength to stay true to your real desires.

I had a parent who loved me unconditionally. He loved me, Betty. I may have not been his favorite, but he loved me for me. This helped me to learn how to follow my dreams. And I want to pass this along to you as well.

The direction may become clouded, the way not clear. But with every beam of light you can get back on track. Trust your way; never let anyone dictate to you what choices you should make; let your own voice guide you. You will need to trust in your journey; with every decision it will give you the confidence to move forward. Let your life unfold; don't try to put yourself in the future because it will unfold and you'll be astonished at the direction you have taken. In my wildest dreams, I could not have ever imagined living in Alabama again; but I'm here and my future never looked brighter.

The decisions you make along the way do not have to be permanent. Be willing to change course when you see that the results of your decision are not in tune with your real desires, your real direction, your GPS. And sure, things will happen in your life that you have no control of. But it is the process in your journey that makes you who you are. Your life experience will capture your heart and be the engine of your soul.

Follow your dreams: the direction may become clouded and unclear, but with every gleam of light that comes, get back on track. Trust your way: never let anyone dictate to you what choices you should make; let you voice guide you. Trust in your journey: with every decision it will give you the confidence to move forward. Let your life unfold: don't try to put yourself in the future. It will happen, and you'll be astonished. The decisions you make along the way do not have to be permanent. Be willing to change course when you that see the results of a decision are not in line with your values and your thinking. Things will happen in your life that you have no control over; it is the process of your journey that makes you who you are. Your life experience will capture your heart and fuel the engine of your soul.

Work with what you've got. Never ... Ever ... Give ... Up ... Your ... Dream! Your dreams are yours to nurture with action and yours to grow ... and they will grow only if you believe. The wounds of your past—rape, molestation, whippings for "stepping out of place," not being allowed to show anger or cry afterwards—these things damaged your self-esteem. Yet through it all, you've held on to a belief in God and God's belief in you.

Here are some words of wisdom that have helped me over the years:

Often the difference between a successful person and a failure is not one has better abilities or ideas, but the courage that one has to bet on one's ideas, to take a calculated risk and to act. —Maxwell Maltz

The most important thing in life is not the triumph but the struggle. The essential thing is not to have conquered but to have fought well. —Pierre de Courbertin

Life's not about waiting for the storm to pass. It's about learning to dance in the rain. —Vivian Greene

The future you see is the future you get. —Robert G. Allen: Canadian-American businessman and author

Knowing is not enough; we must apply. Wishing is not enough; we must do. —Johann Von Goethe

A stumbling block to the pessimist is a stepping stone to the optimist. —Eleanor Roosevelt

What lies behind us and what lies before us are tiny matters compared to what lies within us. —Ralph Waldo Emerson

Never give up on a dream just because of the time it will take to accomplish it. The time will pass anyway. —Earl Nightingale, American motivational speaker and author

Everything you want is just outside your comfort zone. —Robert G. Allen, bestselling author and renowned financial advisor

Keep away from small people who try to belittle your ambitions. Small people always do that, but the really great make you feel that you, too, can become great. —Mark Twain

Don't be afraid of your fears. They're not there to scare you. They're there to let you know that something is worth it. —C. JoyBell

Nothing can stop the man with the right mental attitude achieving his goal; nothing on earth can help the man with the wrong mental attitude. —Thomas Jefferson

Nobody can go back and start a new beginning, but anyone can start today and make a new ending. —Maria Robinson

Someone was hurt before you, wronged before you, hungry before you, frightened before you, beaten before you, humiliated before you, raped before you ... yet, someone survived. ... You can do anything you choose to do. —Maya Angelou

You're braver than you believe, and stronger than you seem, and smarter than you think. —A. A. Milne

Our truest life is when we are in dreams awake. — Henry David Thoreau

Don't think about making life better for other people who don't even deserve you, rather, focus on making your life the best, for yourself and those who love you. —C. Joy Bell

Believe in yourself and all that you are. Know that there is something inside you greater than any obstacle. — Christian D. Larson

About Betty Tucker:

A native of Troy, Alabama, Betty Tucker has a degree in behavioral science from the University of San Francisco. She also has a Clear Multiple Subject Teaching Credential. She worked for nineteen years with the U.S. Postal Service and for nineteen years with the San Francisco Unified School District. She has five children and four grandchildren and now lives in Richmond, California, and in Montgomery, Alabama. Thank you for your consideration.

Made in the USA
Lexington, KY
03 July 2018